WHAT'S YOUR PLAN ?

A Pathway to Writing and Publishing Your Work

Alberta Lampkins

A.L. Savvy Publications
P.O. Box 30203
Clarksville, TN 37040
http://alsavvypublications.com

Copyright © 2015 by Alberta Lampkins

All rights reserved. This book may not be reproduced in whole or in part or transmitted in any form or by any means, electronic or mechanical, including photocopy, recording, or any information storage and retrieval system, without permission in writing from the publisher, A.L. Savvy Publications, P.O. Box 30203, Clarksville, TN 37040.

ISBN 13: 978-0-9903805-4-2
ISBN 13: 978-0-9903805-5-9 (eBook)

Cover design: WWW.MICHAHDSGNS.COM

A.L. Savvy Publications can bring Alberta Lampkins to your live event. For more information or to book an event, contact A.L. Savvy Publications at 931-257-8530 or email Alberta Lampkins at Alberta@alsavvypublications.com or visit the website at http://alsavvypublications.com.

DEDICATION

This book is dedicated to all the aspiring writers who need a little encouragement and guidance along their writing journey.

CONTENTS

	Acknowledgments	i
1	Introduction	1
2	What's your writing style?	Pg # 3
3	Writing Space	Pg # 7
4	What's your genre?	Pg # 9
5	Are you writing a novel, novella or a short story?	Pg # 15
6	What about your work?	Pg # 17
	-Tips on Dialogue	Pg # 21
	-Writing tips	Pg # 23
	-Putting it all together	Pg # 25
7	What about building your writing skills?	Pg # 27
8	Self-editing do's and don'ts	Pg # 39
9	Publishing methods	Pg # 47
10	What about marketing your book?	Pg # 55
11	What about Public Relations?	Pg # 63
12	Sample Articles	Pg # 67
13	Sample Business Plan	Pg # 79
14	Sample Press Release	Pg # 93
15	Descriptive word list	Pg # 97
16	About the author	Pg # 175

ACKNOWLEDGMENTS

Heartfelt thanks to my husband and my family for allowing me time to pursue my dream and share all that I have learned with others.

What's Your Plan?
A Pathway to Writing and Publishing Your Work

So you want to be a writer? You want to see your name boldly printed on the front of an amazing book: your book, right? Then what's your plan? How are you going to bring your brilliant words to print? It starts with you - dare to dream and design a well thought-out plan of action and make it happen! Whether you want to write an incredible account or your family's history, a killer cookbook, the next Harry Potter style series or a book of poetry honoring the beloved Maya Angelou, you can do it. You have the ability to bring your vision to life and share your words with the world. Believe in yourself - that's the first step.

It took me years to get enough courage to become a writer. And even when I finished my first manuscript, I let self-doubt prevent me from moving forward. My story sat on pages in a pile. I lugged my words around from place to place as

I moved about with my military spouse. As an avid reader, I attended book conferences, and as an aspiring writer, I attended writing seminars and attended creative writing classes. Nothing propelled my writing forward, until I realized, I was the only person holding me back. The power is within.

The art of forming great literature starts with an idea, a thought and a vision. The goal: to give an account of an event or story that is either true or fictitious that either entertains, informs or enlightens readers. We all have a story in us and many of us want to share it. If the writer in you is burning to come out and you want to weigh all your options, read along and the hope is for you to prepare to move forward with publishing your work. This book will give an overview of the publishing arena and highlight approaches to self-publishing. Whichever method you choose, the most important point is that you have a plan, pursue your dream and never give up.

"There is no greater agony than bearing an untold story inside you." -**Maya Angelou**

What's Your Writing Style?

Are you the Subject Matter Expert? Well then, your writing style may fit Expository Writing. Expository writing is a subject-oriented writing style, in which the main focus of the author is to tell you about a given topic or subject, and leave out personal opinions. Pertinent facts and information that explains something in the process is typical for this style of writing. The subject matter expert, as I define it, enjoys the thrill of writing "How-to" articles and books sharing facts. Expository writer's mission is to share something they believe has meaning and purpose to readers and sometimes, to the world. If this is you, gather all your facts and start writing that book that will enlighten eagerly awaiting bookworms.

Are you the Detective? Okay, your writing style is most likely Descriptive Writing. Descriptive writing is a style of writing which focuses on describing a character, and event or a place in great detail. The author specifies details of events rather than just give the information of that event which happened. The Detective, as I call this type of writer, describes places, people, events, situations or locations in a detailed way. The author captures what he or she sees, hears, tastes, and feels in their writing. It is almost poetic at times reading the descriptions created by writers. Grounded in matters of observation or experiences, descriptive writers are informative, detailed and talented in "showing," not just telling a story.

Say, are you the Lawyer? Well, not an actual lawyer, but your writing style sure is persuasive. Persuasive writing is a type of writing which contains justifications and reasons to make someone believe on the point the writer is talking about. Persuasive writing contains the opinions, biasness and justification of the author. Persuading and convincing the reader on their point of view. The Lawyer, as I purposely nicknamed, or a.k.a, the persuasive writer, gives reason, arguments and justifications for their characters and makes the reader believe their point of view. These writers have a knack for cleverly persuading readers to like, even unlikable characters. The stories they write often are compelling, convincing, effective and satisfying. Maybe you are the next Lawyer, well, persuasive writer, to win over readers with your intriguing characters. Go for it!

Could you be the Witness? If you are the one telling what happened to everyone in the story, then you are likely a Narrative writer. Narrative writing is a type of writing in which the author places himself as the character and narrates to you the story. Novels, short stories, novellas, poetry and biographies generally fall under the wings of the narrative writing style. Most all narrative writing has characters and dialogues in it, usually consisting of plots with situations of action, conflict, emotional events, problems and an end solution. The witness, as I so kindly call it, masters the art of narration and guides the reader along the story line. You are in the heads of all your characters and a witness to their secrets, schemes and actions. First person narrative means writing from the "I" point of view. Third person narrative form is writing from the omniscient point of view. Here you use he/she form. Second-person narrative form is the least-used form in novels; it is the "you" point of view. People are ready to curl up on the couch with a cup of tea and a warm blanket to read what you have to tell them about your characters. Get to writing!

Maybe you fit more than one style of writing ...and that is okay, you just have to at least know what you're writing style is. Different readers have different ideas of what makes a good book, therefore, the author has to write in the style that fits best for them. Often, deciding the writing style that's right is determined by your audience, your personal style of speech, and where your writing will be available. Think about who will be reading your writing, the medium through which you will publish your writing and your "natural" style of writing. If you try to imitate others in your writing, you may be setting yourself up for a "hung jury" or better yet, a writing disaster. Find your niche and **represent your style**.

Writing Space

Find your own personal space to write. There are different ideas on what represents a great writing space. What works well for one writer may be completely opposite for another. A fantastic writing space may be at home, at the office, a coffee shop, a park or a noisy restaurant. It depends on what space inspires YOU to write. Finding the perfect spot may have a lot to do with who you are. Are you an "Early-riser" writer? A "Noon"-writer? A "Late-night" writer? An "All-night" writer? Or are you a "Squeeze-in-when-you-can" writer? Dependent on how you answer this question may tell a lot about where you will lay claim to your writing hub. Whichever space you choose to scribe, make sure it will entice you to be sure-footed, disciplined and consistent.

Here are a few suggestions to create a perfect writing zone:

1. Cozy, comfortable and inspirational spot with a good surface to write on (desk, table, etc.).

2. Simple, clean and clutter free.
3. Have all your essential writing tools: IPad, laptop or computer, writing pad, note cards, sticky notes, pens, pencils, thesaurus and a good cup of coffee, tea or water.
4. A view with a window, natural lighting, a motivational quote, art or a scene with limited distractions.
5. A place that is quiet or has the sounds of soft music or a place where you can tune out the noise around you and focus on your writing.
6. A spot with the freedom to be you and ignite your innermost thoughts and creativity!

What's Your Genre?

A genre is a style of expressing yourself in writing. And there are plenty different types of genre. It can be difficult for a new writer to find themselves falling under one genre or another. However, knowing what genre best suits your writing is very helpful and quite frankly, necessary. Readers look for books within a certain genre. They have an easier time finding your book, if labeled to be of a certain type of genre. Choosing a genre that fits you will help you to target your desired audience, connect with your readers and market your book. Your book is unique and though you may not think it deserves a label, it does. If you have a hard time figuring out what genre your book fits in, find books that are similar to your style and see where they are shelved in the bookstores. This should help. Here is list of some popular genres; however, you may find a broader selection and a varied definition.

Adventure fiction: stories in which characters are involved in dangerous and/or exhilarating exploits.

Allegory: a story using symbolism to express truths about the human condition.

Autobiography: a history of a person's life, written or told by that person, often written in narrative form of the person's life.

Biography: a written account of another person's life.

Christian fiction: is writing that deals with Christian themes and incorporates the Christian world view.

Comedy: a story with elements and situations intended to amuse.

Comedy-drama: a story with both humorous and serious elements.

Detective fiction: stories based on the commission and/or investigation of wrongdoing.

Drama: stories composed in verse or prose, usually for theatrical performance, where conflicts and emotion are expressed through dialogue and action.

Epic: originally a long poem celebrating the

exploits of a factual or fictitious hero, but now applied to prose works on the same level as well.

Detective fiction: stories in which the protagonist investigates a crime.

Fantasy fiction: stories involving imaginary beings in the real world or in an alternate reality and assuming suspension of disbelief about magic and/or supernatural powers.

Fiction: a narrative literary works whose content is produced by the imagination and is not necessarily based on fact.

Fictional biography: a story structured to resemble a factual life story.

Folklore: are songs, stories, myths, and proverbs of a person of "folk" handed down by word of mouth. Folklore is a genre of literature widely held, but false and based on unsubstantiated beliefs.

Genre fiction: stories intended to appeal to readers because of adherence to a specific formula (such as adventure fiction or detective fiction), rather than on their literary merits.

Gothic fiction: stories often taking place in an isolated setting and involving strange and/or perilous happenings.

Historical fiction: a story with fictional characters and events in a historical setting.

Horror fiction: stories incorporating supernatural and/or inexplicable elements and intended to arouse fear and dread.

Melodrama: a story that emphasizes action over characterization and features exaggerated dramatic plot elements.

Mystery fiction: stories that detail the solution of a crime or other wrongdoing.

Non-fiction: Informational text dealing with an actual, real-life subject. This includes biographies, history, essays, speech, and narrative non-fiction.

Poetry: is verse and rhythmic writing with imagery that evokes an emotional response from the reader.

Romance: a love story, also a tale taking place in a distant time and place and involving adventure with often supernatural or mysterious elements.

Romantic comedy: a lighthearted story detailing a romance and its complications.

Satire: a story that pokes fun at human

shortcomings such as arrogance, greed and vanity.

Science fiction: stories focusing on how science and technology affect individuals and civilizations.

Short stories: fiction of such briefness cannot support subplots.

Thriller: a dramatic story punctuated with action, adventure, and suspense.

Tragedy: a story with a catastrophic and/or unfortunate outcome.

Tragicomedy: a story with both humorous and heartbreaking aspects.

Urban fiction: also known as street lit, or gangsta fiction, is a literary genre set, as the name implies, in a city landscape; however, the genre is defined by the socio-economic realities and culture of its characters as the urban setting. The tone for urban fiction is usually dark, focusing on the underside of city living.

...

Are you writing a novel, novella or a short story?

Determining how many pages composes a novel, novella, novelette, short story or a long story can be knotty. Miriam-Webster dictionary on-line defines a **novel**: a long written story usually about imaginary characters and events or an invented prose narrative that is usually long and complex and deals especially with human experience through a usually connected sequence of events. A **novella**: a story with a compact and pointed plot or a work of fiction intermediates in length and complexity between a short story and a novel. A **novelette**: a novella. A **short story**: an invented prose narrative shorter than a novel usually dealing with a few characters and aiming at unity of effect and often concentrating on the creation of a mood rather than a plot. And a **long story**: a short story of more than average length: a prose narrative intermediate between a short story and a short novel.

Different publishers, writers and people in

general, have different answers to how many pages makes up a novel, novella, etc. The length of a story, called a novel, varies greatly in length. Miriam-Webster only defines each category and does not specify a length for a novel, novella, novelette, short story or long story. Authors, writers, self-publishers, publishing houses and other entities examine the definitions of a novel, novella, novelette, short story and long story and make an educated guess as to which one applies to their specific story.

The most important class is: YOUR story. If you focus on length, as opposed to writing an incredibly great story, then you may lose your readers. Writing to fill pages to say you have written a novel is not good practice. Readers are smart; they will pick up on those pesky pages filled with fluff. Be passionate about your work and if you write a grand story with 20,000 words or 150,000 words, then you have accomplished a notable feat.

What about YOUR work?

Writing is an amazing journey. The author can create fantasy, bring awareness, document history, capture time, share stories and express thoughts and ideas with the power of the pen or pecks on a word processor. Fear also comes with writing. Writer's often wonder: Will anyone read my story? Will readers like my narrative? Will my point come across in my writing? Will I entertain the minds of readers? Will readers appreciate my craft? Will they understand my thoughts, ideas and vision? Will anyone buy my book? We can ask ourselves a million more questions and it will all equate to self-doubt if we allow those questions to lead to giving up.

When you become passionate about writing your book, telling your story and expressing yourself through word, there is no room for uncertainty, hesitation, indecision and doubt. Whether you sell one copy of your book or a million copies, you are accomplished because you did it. You followed your heart and wrote your book. Critics will have their say, but for the best of us, we will applaud you. Just take a look around you; your book WILL be different. You have a vision of the world through your own lens. Write YOUR story. If every author told the same story, the exact same way, people would stop reading. We learn from others. Your experiences may sound different, look different and feel different. That's because you are your own unique story.

Be ready to trample through the trenches, hold grip of your vision and never, ever let anyone deter you from writing. Here are a few secrets to becoming an author.

1. Write, write and then, write. Totally take your writing seriously. Believe in yourself and what your story is about and write what feels right to you.
2. Create an outline and breakdown how your story will unfold. This will help you to see the "big picture" and keep your work flowing in the right direction.

3. Who, what, where, when, why and how are the questions to ask yourself as you are putting your plot and characters together. If you start with a good premise of what your work is about, it will be easy to navigate your way through your writing.
4. Set a writing goal. You will write two to five pages or ten to fifteen pages per day until you reach the end. You will write early mornings or late nights. Whatever fits your comfort level and works best for you, do that. Make sure your goal is realistic and attainable.
5. Write your first draft before letting anyone else's opinion deter you from writing the story you want to tell. After you have finished your draft, then ask for feedback.
6. Read your story aloud to get a feel for how it sounds and how it flows.
7. Edit, re-edit and polish. Tip: Back up your work frequently and even email a copy of your latest version to yourself as an extra precaution.

ALBERTA LAMPKINS

Tips on Dialogue

1. When using dialogue in your writing, a good rule of thumb is: Use one speaker per paragraph. Begin a new paragraph when another person begins to speak.
2. In writing dialogue, the dash [—] is used to show breaks in thought and shifts in tone.
3. Use ellipsis [...] for dialogue that fades away.
4. Don't use colons or semi-colons in dialogue.
5. Use punctuation inside quotation marks.
6. Don't allow your characters to speak more than three sentences in a row without a break.
7. End the dialogue line with a comma if you're adding a dialogue tag (he said, she said, etc.), but with a full stop if you're adding an action.

Writing Tips

1. *Use active voice rather than passive voice.* In active voice, the subject of the sentence performs the action of the verb on an object. In passive voice, the object appears as the subject of the sentence.

   Thousands of tourists visit Niagara Falls every year. (Active)
   Niagara Falls is visited by thousands of tourists every year. (Passive)

2. *Do not overuse "there is...there was," "it is...it was," etc.*

   Example: There was a child laughing in the theater.
   Better: A child laughed in the theater.

3. *Use words like "said" or "asked" for speaker tags.* Speaker tags are the words used to describe speech. Characters can't "sigh" or "smile" their dialogue.

   Example: "I love you," Harriet sighed.
   Better: "I love you," Harriet said with a sigh.

4. *Use adverbs scarcely.* Instead, rely on strong verbs to move the action.

   Example: "Get in here," she said furiously.
   Better: "Get in here." She scowled at him.

5. *Use precise language rather than vague language. Using vague language weakens writing.*

   Example: The restaurant is kind of dark.
   Better: The restaurant is too dark, I can't see the words on the menu.

6. *Stay away from dangling modifiers.* When a clause introduces a sentence, it needs to have the same subject as the sentence itself.

   Example: After reading the great new book, the movie based on it is sure to be *electrifying.*
   Better: After reading the great new book, Alberta thought the movie based on it was sure to be electrifying.

Putting it all together

1. Write an outstanding first paragraph that grabs the reader's attention.
2. Develop your characters.
3. Choose a point of view.
4. Write meaningful dialogue.
5. Distinguish setting and background.
6. Set up the plot.
7. Create conflict and tension.
8. Build to a crisis or climax.
9. Deliver a resolution.
10. Review, revise and edit...then edit again.

ALBERTA LAMPKINS

What about building your writing skills?

Have you thought about writing an article, writing for a blog or entering literary contests or journaling? These are just a few ways to build your writing skills. Elevating your writing skills will allow you to advance in a writing world where your point of view is important. Becoming a great writer doesn't happen by chance. You have to continually polish your writing skills to stay ahead in the literary world. Even the most prolific writers continue to work toward improving upon their gift. As a new writer, it is extremely important to sparkle and one way is to build a writing portfolio.

Many major industry magazines, newspapers, community newspapers, blogs, and small press magazines are looking for creative article ideas to feature on their platform. They are looking for fresh ideas, new topics and imaginative slants to basic topics. You can write about self-help, how-to, life experiences, current events, about a person in your community, a funny story, other writers or your thoughts on gun control. The possibilities are endless! Pitch your idea to your favorite magazine or research blogs you like and post your point of view. Follow the submission guidelines to your prospective magazine or blog and keep at it. Every "quality" written work you compose will vastly increase your success as a writer.

Here is an article I wrote for BOLD Favor Magazine. BOLD Favor Magazine, the flagship communication for the Leading Through Living Community, highlights BOLD and fearless people, organizations, and causes. http://www.boldfavormagazine.com.
The article appeared in the December 2014 Issue.

The Importance of Being Social

Creating valuable social networking relationships is significant. As we near the year 2020 of the 21st Century, one might ask the question, are we growing closer socially or farther away from each other? Smart technology has become a part of our daily lives and our increasingly mobile world has given rise to social networks. Google, Facebook, LinkedIn, Twitter, Instagram and emerging new social connections have changed the way people and businesses interact. We are now an interconnected world. What does that mean? With one touch, we can reach humankind across the globe. Information about whom we are, the mission and goals of our business, our brand and products are in the grasp of the world. We are reshaped by the ways we communicate with each other, from customers, business associates, friends to our family. More change is inevitable. New technologies and "on-the- spot" information will look even more differently by 2020. Over the long run, we will have a "smarter" world; however, will the need to be social evaporate?

Talking to people, making connections and developing a rapport with individuals are not a dying concept. It is in fact, important. Sharing knowledge, experience, personal struggles, resources and having ambassadors to help promote who you are is vital. Getting to know the right people who can help you reach your goal and attract the right partnerships cannot be totally replaced by a "smart" world. We trust what we can hear, see, touch and feel. We trust our instincts and when we meet someone face-to-face, our opinions change based on what we observe about that person. Intelligent data and analytical computing is a great asset, but the human brain and the human heart are far more advanced than any smart device. Reading about Oprah Winfrey's success, watching her television shows and following her on Twitter, is quite different from actually meeting Oprah, talking to Oprah, sharing thoughts and ideas and building a bond to help advance each forward.

Invitations to the right events in our lives and exposure to the right people help to increase the circle of influence in our business and personal dealings. Getting to know and understand other people's perspectives help to foster new ideas, new insights and new wisdom. The right exposure is invaluable. We can send out a thousand different tweets and post every day on Facebook, and granted, we may find some success in whatever it is we are trying to promote, however, the right information in the hands of the right person who has met you, heard your pitch or studied the way you carry yourself, may make the world of difference.

There is an importance of being social. We must not let a "smart" world take us away from getting out and meeting new prospects, encouraging others, sharing thoughts, promoting ideas, networking and making personal connections. We are already equipped with the most valuable tools we need, our beautiful minds and our hearts. Let's enrich each other by taking advantage of new age technology, but never letting go of our humanity.

Another article I wrote for Black Pearls Magazine, winner of the 2013 and 2014 Best Literary Magazine Award Presented by the 10th Annual African American Literary Awards Show. The article appeared in the January 2015 Issue.

Am I, a Fixer?

By Alberta Lampkins

I do enjoy putting into action my problem-solving skills and helping others to see the value of their lives. Maybe it's a gift or a calling – whichever one it is, it has been of enormous help to my life. I have a built-in aspiration to be better and I like to inspire, encourage and support others to enjoy their journey in life and follow their dreams. I live in the moment and I am grateful for the splendor of each episode. Each new day gives us an opportunity to learn something new or do something different, why not invite others to share your faith and confidence that what God has done for one, he may do even better for you. No one can drive you but you. However, enthusiasm is transmittable and I thrive on energizing people around me. My faith allows me to walk in the steps of optimism and see the world through a glass that is half full and not half empty.

I believe that those we encounter in our day-to-day lives were meant to be there for some reason or another. Life is connected for a purpose and if it is not to uplift each other, then maybe it's for us to learn a lesson and move on. Supporting other's budding ambition leads right into guiding me towards my own personal discovery. I'm not cramped by societal standards and I overlook flaws and look for the beauty in each person I meet. They may be the reflection of God, he wants me to see. I'm grateful for a forgiving heart and a loving soul toward human kind.

My earliest mentors were my parents. I remember dancing and singing in front of the mirror as a girl and my father smiled. He said I sang and danced well, though I'm not so sure I was really in tune or in rhythm. But his smile and his words of encouragement made me feel like I could dance or sing. A brown girl from an urban neighborhood in Buffalo, New York could be whatever she wanted to be because, not only did her father tell her that, but her mother did as well. I never became a dancer or a singer; however, I've pursued my dreams and continue to live a life knowing that I can do whatever I will with faith, hard work and dedication. I believe anyone can achieve their goals in life and sometimes it just takes someone to encourage them along the way.

A grade school teacher paid the remaining balance of my field trip to New York City after my father passed and never asked for a penny of it back. She believed I had potential and wanted to give me the opportunity to experience culture. A supervisor wrote me a note thanking me for joining her staff – she believed I would make a good social worker one day. I met a stranger, who after a brief introduction, shared her story of struggle with depression and I listened and I told her what I saw in her – she said she believed we met for a reason and she felt better that day.

Am I, a Fixer? The definition of a fixer is a

person whose actions and opinions strongly influence the course of events. Not sure if that directly fits me, however I do like to find solutions to obstacles holding people from moving towards success in life. If I have said a word of encouragement that sparked an action and helped someone foster their goal or to see life in a bigger and brighter light, then I count it as paying it forward.

■ ■ ■

Writing a newsletter for your church, local organization, book club, work group or you name it, is another way to improve your writing skills. Determine if you want to write a weekly, bi-weekly, monthly or quarterly newspaper and consider the audience your newsletter will capture. List topics to write about and develop a plan. Write about topics that will be of interest to your readers. Whether you are writing a family newsletter or writing for a group of soccer moms, it all adds up to enhancing your writing skills.

Short story and creative writing contests

and competitions can lead to impressive opportunities for writers. If you Google creative writing contests and competitions, you will be amazed at the huge amount of writing opportunities out there on the world wide web. Polish up your work, send out your best entry and see what happens. This may be the perfect setting to store and display your masterpiece. You will increase your writing skills, meet other creative writers, get a glimpse of other writers work, and add value to your writing profile. Many writing contests and competitions offer sizable cash prizes. Entry fees, submissions and general guidelines vary from contest to contest. It will be worth the research to find the right competition for you and submit your work. Here is a list of some types of writing contests out there:

Sitcom Writing Contest

Screenplay Writing Contest

Poetry Writing Contest

Satirist Comedy Writing Contest

Love Story Writing Contest

Romantic Poetry Writing Contest

Ocean Dream Cruise Liner Writing Contest

Short Story Writing Contest
Amazon Novel Contest
Dayton National Story Contest
Halloween Poetry Writing Contest
EBook Writing Contest
Fiction Writing Contest
Nonfiction Writing Contest
Songwriting Contest

An effective and highly ingenious way to grow as a writer is to journal. It can make a big difference in your life, not just as a writer, but even on a more personal level. You can say what's really on your mind with no intended audience. Capturing your thoughts of the moment and tidbits of life may lead to brilliant ideas for a novel down the line. Journaling is easy. There are no deadlines, no rules, uncensored writing and there is room for mistakes. Journaling is liberating. Not worrying about grammar, point of view or plot can be relaxing and stress free.

Basically, you are keeping a record of your thoughts, ideas and memories. You can write about the banana sitting on your desk or the phone call you received from a friend. There are no limitations to your thoughts. Journaling brings out honesty and helps free your writing capabilities. In a way, journaling helps you to take note of the world around you – you become observant and more reflective in your script. Writing a message or thought anywhere from one word to a thousand or more in your journal, may just help you develop into the most amazing writer you can be.

Try it- you have nothing to lose and only a world of written thoughts to gain!

ALBERTA LAMPKINS

Self-Editing Do's and Don'ts

Do approach self-editing as laborious and unavoidable. Your reputation as a writer is on the line and you must prepare to work tirelessly to produce a well written masterpiece. Self-editing is a tough grind but with dedication and unwavering perseverance it can be done well.

Do invest in grammar and style books and resources. Becoming a good writer requires that YOU understand the mechanics of grammar. Knowing about grammar is important because it helps to find the language to get the point across clear, precise and effectively.

Here are a few helpful resources:

-Merriam-Webster's Collegiate Dictionary

-Merriam-Webster Online

-The Chicago Manual of Style 16

-Webster's New World English Grammar Handbook

-Guide to Grammar and Style, by Jack Lynch, Rutgers University (On-line)

-Self-Edit Your Novel, by David H. Fears

-On Writing Well, by William Zinsser

-Grammar Girl's Quick and Dirty Tips for Better Writing, by Mignon Fogarty

-How to Avoid 10 Punctuation Mistakes, by Mitchell Euan

-The Writer's Handbook, Clear, Concise, Sentences (On-line)

Do read your manuscript out loud and/or have someone else read it to you. Reading out loud forces you to read each word and let you hear how the words sound together. When you read silently or too hurriedly, you may hop over errors or make unconscious adjustments.

Do have more than one round of editing and revising. Focus on the different elements of your manuscript...it is hard to insure that details connect with just a quick review. In a way, editing is building on what you did well and taking your manuscript to the next level. You may have to edit, revise, edit and then revise again until YOU have reached your personal standard and YOU feel good about it.

Don't be tempted to take the easy way out

and ignore editing and revising your work. It took a lot of get-up-and-go to complete your first draft, don't bail out on seeing it through to the end. Editing and revising will get you to the finish line as a winner.

Don't do it all yourself. Ask for help. Your work is personal, precious and you want to protect it. You also want your work to be pleasingly profitable and polished. Having a friend or someone else take a second look at your work can be very helpful. If you prefer to use someone not close to you, you may choose a beta reader. A beta reader is a person (usually non-professional) who reads a work of fiction with a critical eye, with the aim of improving grammar, spelling, characterization, and general style of a story before its release to the public.

Most importantly, don't give up!

On a personal note, self-editing my first novel, *Teach Me How To Fly*, tragically ended in failure. I believed my story would over-power the blaring mistakes and somehow my novel would be in the hands of Oprah or some great and mighty book lover. I believed no editor would do my story justice and I did not want to have a random person with expertise turn my white pages into oceans of red ink. So, I read every book I could find on writing and then purchased *The Write Writer* editing software. I just knew this editing software would save me hundreds of dollars and drop the need of a trained eye.

Wrong! The software captured grammar rule violations and common mistakes; however, plot and point-of-view were left solely up to me. It all seemed okay, until I blindly plunged into the sea of truth and reality opened my eyes. A great story with blaring mistakes which distracted readers. I had a choice, live with the mistakes or redeem my credibility and fix my blunder. I invested in an editor, took the time to revise my novel and re-released, *Teach Me How To Fly.*

Finding a helpful and affordable editor can be a difficult task, especially for those writers planning to self-publish. The cost of editing can be astronomical and many editing services are impersonal. The author may have paid a hefty price for a well edited manuscript, but no personal connection with the editor evolved. It is important to find an editor who is familiar with your genre or writing style. Freelance editors are one way to go, their fees may be reasonable and their work more personal. However, finding a skillful freelance editor will require good quality research. Many freelance editors may be found on platforms like Twitter, Facebook and Instagram, as well as other social media sites. Word of mouth may be the best option. Network with other writers and find out their experiences with editors and their recommendations.

Depending on what your editing needs are, here is a guideline to common editing services available on the market:

Substantial Editing – is an intensive form of editing. It involves a manuscript or document to be reviewed as a whole. The editor will generally rewrite portions of the document. The editor may rearrange, delete, add, and reword entire pages and chapters to improve the structure or content of the manuscript. Substantial editing may be time consuming and costly, however, highly effective for writers.

Copy Editing – is the most common form of editing. The editor corrects problems of grammar, style, repetition, word usage, and jargon. Editors may adjust sentences and paragraph structure, drop redundant words, and replace repetitive words or weak words. Copy editors may correct mechanical, syntax, style and usage errors. This type of editor will read from the point of view of the intended audience and make sure the manuscript is logical and consistent.

Proofreading – a very basic form of editing. The editor will review and correct basic grammatical and spelling errors. Minor errors corrected may include: errors of grammar and style, errors of capitalization, punctuation, spelling and word usage.

Line Editing – The editor reads and scouts out plot inconsistencies and factual errors. The editor reviews line by line and word by word.

Fact Checking – a fact checker insures the validity of facts or quotes in a document or conducts research to correct the facts. This type of editing may review the document for cultural sensitivities, or political, moral or ethical strong views.

Ghost Writer – a professional writer or editor, who writes for and gives the credit of authorship to another, their name is often not attached to the written work.

Formatting – A formatter will modify a document to insure it fits the proper format for various publications. This may include adjusting the page size, margins, page numbering, adding titles or styles to graphic outlines.

ALBERTA LAMPKINS

Publishing Methods

Now that you have honed in on your writing style, selected the genre for your literary work, written your first draft, revised, edited and finally finished your book, it is time to look at how you will publish your masterpiece. There are different types of book publishing methods for every type of writer, varying primarily on the market for your manuscript. Knowing the different types of publishers will be helpful as you turn your dream of being an author into reality.

Traditional Trade Book Publishers – acquire, edit, produce, publish and sell the books through established channels, including libraries, wholesalers and bookstores. Each Traditional or Trade publisher, generally, publishes books in a broad variety of formats (hardcover, trade paperback, mass market paperback, e-books, audiobooks), and in a sizeable assortment of topics and genres. These companies produce books designed for the general public. The big five

Trade Book Publishers are: Hachette Book Group, Harper Collins, MacMillan Publishers, Penguin Random House and Simon and Schuster.

Book Developers/Book Creator– is companies specializing in creating books published under the imprint of a trade publisher. The book developer often creates the idea for the book or series of books and then hands off the concept to a publisher. Developers work with authors, primarily self-published authors, helping them to bring their work to print. Book Developers manages everything from editing, to designing the book, to getting in printed. Some book developers also prepare query letters, build websites and create other promotional tools. The book developer is the "behind the scenes" person working for the author. Many self-published authors and small presses use book developers.

Scholarly and Professional Publishers – produce a variety of academic textbooks, workbooks, reference books, scholarly and professional journals in a diverse range of fields. Another name for this type of publishing is STM - brief for scientific, technical and medical publishing. Many professional publishers market to colleges, scholars, professionals, libraries, and general readers.

Independent Publishers, Small press, Indie publishers – are classically smaller, privately held publishing companies. Independent publishers typically publish an array of books, and many specialize in specific genres.

Overall, Independent Publishers cover a wide arena of titles, from children's books to women's empowerment, music, arts, fantasy, fiction, non-fiction and a multitude of other books and genres. Some operate with a reach as big as a traditional publishing house. Independent publishers are keenly involved in the book selection process – editing, marketing and distribution. A contract is made with the author, often paying royalties. Independent publishers own the copies they have printed, but typically do not own the copyright to the book itself. There are over a hundred major independent book publishers in the United States and others abroad.

Self-Publishers – are do-it-yourself companies that give authors the power to create their book and see their work in print. Primarily, self-published authors use print-on-demand (POD) technology to get their books in the hands of readers. Self-publishers are responsible for every part of the publishing process (Editing, book cover design, ISBN numbers, marketing, printing and shipping cost, distribution, etc.). The costs can vary from minimum upfront cost to thousands of dollars. The author has complete creative control and retains the rights to their book.

*Self-Publishing tip – If you choose to self-edit your work, be sure to read books on writing, participate in creative writing courses, use peer review writing websites and get professional feedback. You are the best agent for your book and your "brand" is on the line. There are more options than ever before for self-publishers and you are in control of your writing destiny. Don't be afraid to step out in the self-publishing arena…just be well prepared.

It is important **copyright** your work. Copyrights helps make your work your exclusive property. Whether you publish on a blog, a newspaper, a magazine, or in book form, this is another method to establish you as the original author. Be sure that when published, the work contains your full name, the date of publication and the copyright symbol. Official copyright registration is necessary. To register your work with the United States Copyright office, go to **www.copyright.gov**. The site will walk you through the registration process. The current fee to register your work is $35.00.

As a self-published author, you also want to own your ISBN (International Standard Book Number). It is a unique number assigned to a book title by its publisher for tracking and ordering purposes. If you don't own the ISBN, you do not own all the complete rights to your book. The first three numbers of the ISBN identify the industry (books, publishing). **The next number** is the language group identifier (the language the book is written in), **the next set of**

numbers identifies the publisher, **the next set of numbers** indicates the *book title* and **the last number** is the check digit. **You need one ISBN for your paperback and a different ISBN for the eBook version of your paperback. You will need a third ISBN if you print a hardcover version of the same book.** You will need a bar code for paperback and hard cover books for purchase. You do not need a bar code for eBooks.

The ISBN contains within it a "publisher identifier." This enables anyone to locate the publisher of any particular book or edition. Owning your own ISBNs gives you the ability to control the record for your book. To purchase your own ISBN's, you may contact the United States ISBN Agency at ISBN.org by Bowker. The site will walk you through the purchasing process. The cost varies based upon the number of ISBN numbers and bar codes you need.

Vanity Presses – offer more independence for the author than do mainstream publishing industry; however, their fees can be higher than the fees normally charged for similar printing services, and require restrictive contracts. Writers pay all the publishing costs, including editing, printing and promoting the book. Some vanity presses set the retail price for the book, re-use previous book cover and interior designs, purchase ISBN numbers, offer the author a discount to buy their own book and even hold rights to the book.

ALBERTA LAMPKINS

What about marketing your work?

After you have whipped your manuscript in shape, edited your work and created or purchased services for a professional looking cover, now it is time to prepare to market your book. As I began learning about the writing and publishing world, shock and amazement took over me. I could not believe what I learned from a traditionally published author published. She marketed herself. She explained that although backed by her traditional publisher, she still had to do the work to sell her books. Being a part of a main stream publishing company guaranteed her some exposures and the ability to have her books on the shelf in major book stores, like Barnes & Noble, but pretty much after that, she had to hit the pavement getting her work in the hands of the readers. I studied her, as well as a few other authors I had the privilege of meeting, and I learned what they did to get their work out to the world. I soon realized authors backed by traditional publishers, did the same kind of marketing a dedicated self-publisher did to get their work out to readers.

Whether you take the self-publishing route or pursue traditional publishing, you really are in control and no one will work harder at promoting your work than you. Technology is ever evolving and available to take advantage. Social media platforms are cultivated daily and can be a huge plus for branding and marketing your work. Posting to every form of social media to authors and readers is a great beginning. First you must know your target market.

Definition: *A specific group of consumers at which a company aims its products and services.*
☐

Demographics: What is your target audience's gender, age, race or ethnicity, family structure, household income, employment, and education level?

Geography: What is that person's location, language spoken, dialect, and climate?

Life cycle: What about lifestyle and life stage?

Culture: What is your reader's urban/rural/suburban/small town, work habits, religious observance, holidays and festivals, activities, recreation, entertainment, and volunteerism situation?

Motivation: What are your target audience's beliefs and desires?

Building a brand takes dedication and perseverance. Researching and defining your target market is a "best practice" strategy for all writers desiring to publish. You must connect with the right people at the right time and place. Learning where to find your market may take some investigative skills. Once you have researched and defined your market, find out what motivates them to buy and read books and where to find them.

A great way to begin finding your target market is to attend conventions, book conferences, book club meetings, and writing functions. Join writing, publishing and other groups in person and on social media platforms.

There are a ton of groups on Facebook alone, not to mention twitter and other platforms.

Here is a list of ways to reach your target market:

- Email/webmail
- Blogs
- Facebook user page, fan page
- Twitter membership and twitter related tools
- Reader groups, such as, Good Reads, Library Things and Gravatar
- Google and Google Plus
- LinkedIn
- Kindle Direct Publishing
- Amazon customer and author profiles
- Smashwords
- Amazon discussion forums
- Pinterest
- Video book trailers
- Video interviews
- Chapter readings
- Book signing/speaking event
- You Tube

Having a brand and a strong product is the key

to building market presence and loyal readership. Having a presence on social media platforms mean that you appear, accessible, in-the-know and in demand. Using social media is about building your brand and you must be available and willing to put yourself and your information out there on the World Wide Web.

When creating a social media platform, such as Facebook, twitter or other resources, be sure to respond to new followers. It is important to stay actively engaged with your followers, however, remain professional always. You do not want to become annoying to your readers. Too many irrelevant tweets and other hashtags may work against you and your brand.

Map out a plan on how long you will spend on the best social media platforms. Use a variety of content, text, images, photos, audio, video, presentations and other creative ideas to keep marketing fresh. Don't be afraid to mix it up, you may be surprised by what may capture a readers interests. Keep up-to-date profiles and post regular messages and conversations.

Building a website or blog helps to give a

professional aspect to your work. Readers and buyers of books come in all different forms and fashion. Some prefer to do business by perusing a website, others rely on reviews by Amazon, Barnes & Noble, etc. Having a presence on line will help gather readers and add to your brand as a writer/author. When building a website for a small business, be sure to find an interesting domain name (could be your name.) Seek quality web hosting, have an attractive professional design or layout theme, a logo, beautiful images, social media links, a blog and information about your books; where to purchase them. Also, let the readers know about your website, speaking engagements and book signing events.

Here are a few additional tips:
- Share great articles you've found or written on your website or blog.
- Thank people personally for following you on twitter or Facebook.
- Respond to comments in a timely manner.
- Post a cover reveal or early cover design for your book.

- Create a profile on Pinterest, add your information, including keywords, website/blog, URL, and a little personal information about the type of books you write. Pin your book cover on the site.
- Create a book trailer. (Take a look at other author's book trailers and get an idea of how you would like your book trailer to look.)
- Make a Power Point presentation or keynote presentation about your book, format it as a video and upload it to You Tube.
- Use tags and keywords...tag words such as authorship, creative writing, fiction, romance, historical fiction, mystery, e-publishing, indie publisher, self-publishing, digital publishing, etc.

What about Public Relations?

Who are you? Create a bio, have a professional photo taken and have a good description of your product ready and handy for anyone wanting to know who you are. A professional eye catching bio and photo will lend way to a great first impression. You will be judged as an author by those that read your work, those who may want to be a writer, and by those seeking an interest in you as a writer. Give them your best face first!

Having interesting material available about your book, your skills and who you are as a writer is important. You have to get the news about your product out there by diverse means. Here are some public relations tips:

- Create a bio kit:
    - Professional bio
    - List of Questions and Answers
    - A good photo
    - List of your books or writings
    - List of your speaking engagements

- Create and send out press releases.
    - Press releases should be recent, interesting and important. Think of a short, but catchy headline.
    - Add hyperlinks, URLs, and web addresses.
    - Have photos available.
    - Follow the Five W's: **W**ho it is about, **W**hat happened, **W**hen it took place, **W**here it happened and **W**hy it happened.
    - Have a press release date, a headline, dateline, a summary, and an "About the Author" bio and contact information.
    - Review sample press releases by other authors and use the format and style that is most impressive to you.
    - Tweet your press release, post on Facebook, your website and send out to newspapers, reporters, blog owners, book reviewers, magazines, radio stations, etc.

- Make your press release clear and brief with just enough elements to catch attention.
  - Don't write in passive voice and be sure to check spelling and grammar.
  - Do regular press releases for book launch, news comments, book updates, announcements, speaking engagements, video releases, blogs etc.
- Telephone reporters to inform them about your book release.
- Network with other writers, bloggers, reporters, book clubs and anyone with a vested interest in your venture. Networking gives credibility, establishes yourself as an expert and brings attention to your work as an author.
- Schedule activities to raise awareness and draw interest in yourself as an author, such as a virtual book launch party on Facebook, a traditional book launch party,

speaking engagements and other creative activities.
- Be a guest on internet radio shows, guest spot on webinars and do interviews for online magazines, blogs etc.
- Be a reader and become the president of your own book club.

You may opt to hire a PR and Media consultant or do your own marketing. Whichever method you choose, prepare to work diligently. Every great writer/author has a well put together marketing plan. Coming up with a marketing plan for each new book or writing venture will get easier over time. Easier...but no less work than any other book project. Along the way you will discover what works best for you and ways to improve. There is always room to improve!

There are more options than ever to write and publish your work. So get started and leave a legacy that you will be proud to call your own. Don't forget to create a business plan. Do your research, read books, speak with others, gather information about writing and publishing trends, mistakes, growth, profitability and cost, as well as a competitor's analysis. You can't fail because You have a great plan!

• • •

On the following pages you will find an article I wrote about my publishing journey, a sample of my business plan, a sample press release and a list of valuable descriptive words for writing. Feel free to add on to the list of descriptive words and take notes on the blank pages at the end of the book. Enjoy!

In The Know How: A BOLD Move into the Publishing World

By Alberta Lampkins

Posted on September 1, 2014September 1, 2014 by BOLD Favor Magazine

Don't wish for it, work for it. That simple adage resonated with me and I thought, I can either spend the rest of my life wishing I would have published a book or wishing I would have started a business, or I could work hard and make it happen. I didn't want to just cross something off my bucket list; I wanted to learn everything about the publishing industry. So I set forth learning how to design a book cover, how to format a book for print and eBooks, how to create a website, a logo, a slogan, how to find a book distributor and how to market my emerging ideas.

Based on all that I discovered and with the support of my husband Al and my family, I put in place a savvy business plan and went to work on my aspiration. I jotted down the very best that could happen as I moved forward with this venture, such as, A.L. Savvy Publications will grow and become one of the largest independent publishing companies in the world, to the very worst that could happen, such as, marketing and inability to attract readers will cause my efforts to establish the business to fail. With the best and worst in mind, I was able to see a clear path and move towards a realistic goal.

Perhaps, I could have followed the traditional way of getting published and sent out hundreds of query letters to publishing houses and agents and wait months for them to respond, however, I chose to follow my gumption and pursue a different path. The publishing industry has been given a face-lift, allowing up-and-coming authors and other established writers to get their books in the hands of readers sooner. With modern computer advances and print on demand companies rising; creative and in the know-how independent publishers, such as me, are given dynamic publishing opportunities. Social media has also pushed the publishing industry forward, birthing a new wave of readership.

Very quickly, I learned that everything does not always work out smoothly, but the bumps and bruises are what helped propel me to the next level. I certainly have more to learn and much room to grow. As I advance, I will bring on board an Editor, Graphic Designer and Marketing Manager. It was a great experience writing my first novel, but editing my own work was painful and may not have been the best choice – effective immediately, I fire myself as Chief Editor. I have a driving ambition to see A.L. Savvy Publications grow and prosper and my hope is to give the readers a creative arts experience guaranteed to uplift, inspire and move them through great written works.

Why Should Anyone Help the Homeless?
By Alberta Lampkins

Why should anyone help the homeless? They chose the condition they're in…they don't really need our help, they probably have a stash of money hidden somewhere and are rich! Is that really a reason to tighten our purse straps and walk by as if their lives don't matter? Regardless of what one may believe to be true or untrue about our fellow American brothers and sisters who lack permanent housing… their lives do matter. Their lives reflect our world. They are our mothers, fathers, brothers, sisters, our children and many of our veterans who fought tirelessly for "our" American freedom. They each have a story. A story, which led them to a shelter for a night, that then turned into one more night, which led to days without a home. Do you know their story? Probably not.

Although, the actual number of homeless men, women, children and families is hard to pin point, it is in fact true that a hefty number of people, especially families, are sleeping in shelters, living in their cars, and taking up residence in tent communities. According to estimates of national data, in the United States, more than 3.5 million people experience homelessness each year. The U.S. Department of Housing and Urban Development, point-in-time study estimated that in 2012, there were 99,894 **chronic** homeless people living in America. The size of the homeless Veterans in 2012 was estimated to be 62,619. According to a 2009 study by the National Center of Family Homelessness, 1 out of every 50 American children is homeless each year.

Something is wrong with this picture. Are we to believe that 3.5 million people chose the condition they're in? Or that those 3.5 million people ALL just want a hand-out and not a hand- up? Some of the major causes of homelessness include:

- Lack of Affordable Housing. The growing gap between wage earnings and the cost of housing in the United States leaves millions of families and individuals unable to meet their basic needs, including food, clothing and shelter.
- Lack of Affordable Medical Care. For a low income to middle income family, a sudden illness, chronic disease, or accident can be

financially devastating and leave individuals and families fighting for daily survival.

- Cuts in Federal Assistance. Elimination of federal assistance for housing programs and social services has challenged the ability to reach the people who are in most need of services. During the 1980s, housing programs were cut down and the homeless population in the United States began to grow. Without the security of federal and state assistance, many of the lowest income people must choose between things like food, medical care, and housing to survive.

- Long-standing issues like, unemployment, mental illness, drug addiction, and alcoholism can elevate situations of low income and poverty and put people at greater risk of homelessness. It is not always one factor, but a number of life factors can play a role in the road to homelessness.

We often label the homeless population and lump them in the same category: they are severely mentally handicap, they do not work, they are lazy and they have given up on life. Hmm...is it really fair to group every homeless woman, man, child or veteran together and assign a certain stigma to them? Does this give us probable cause to turn our nose up, pass them by and not offer any assistance? Well if you are one of millions of people with love and compassion in your heart, there are ways you can help. You may not be able to eliminate their circumstance, but you can help show them that we see them, we care and we are willing to lend a hand.

My book club, the Dazzling Divas Literary Club, an online book club with members from various states, including, Georgia, New York, Colorado, Maryland, North Carolina, Texas, Virginia, Tennessee, and across the world in Italy, recently started a "Dare to Care" campaign. Each book club member has been challenged to volunteer in their prospective state with their local homeless shelter, either feeding the homeless, providing personal hygiene items to those in need or making a donation. We are proud of our initiative and encourage others to do the same.

Ways to help:

- Gather toiletries. Simple items such as a small bottle of lotion, deodorant, mouthwash, hand sanitizer or a shaving kit may provide sustenance to a person in need.

- Drop off food. Most all local homeless shelters or care facilities benefit greatly from receiving food to help feed our homeless population. Locate your community shelter and find out what they need.

- Make donations. Pick an amount and give once a month, once a quarter or even once a year. Your donation, whether small or big, can make a difference to one or many of our fellow homeless population.

- Carry a Homeless Care Kit in Your Car. Fill a re-sealable baggie with basic essentials like: Band-Aids, comb, deodorant, feminine hygiene, gloves, hand warmers, juice box, lip balm, lotion, nail file, power bar, razor, shaving cream, soap, socks, tissues, toothbrush and toothpaste, wash cloth, hand sanitizer, wet-wipes and any other item you believe may be a benefit.

Dare to Care, give a hand-up and together let's make a difference in our world!

Sample Business Plan

Executive Summary

A.L Savvy Publications is an up-and-coming independent publishing company structured by Alberta Lampkins as the sole proprietor. The company is a sophisticated and very versatile company yearning to turn out amazing publications. A.L. Savvy Publications will offer its customers the best and duly notable publications in the self-publishing market. There was a time when aspiring authors had to send out manuscript after manuscript to literary agents and publishers and wait for responses, however, the publishing industry has been re-vamped. Independent Publishers and Print on Demand companies and E-book services are steering the way for budding new authors and other established authors as well. Technology and social media have pushed the publishing industry into a new era and have opened the doors for authors to get their work out to the world more efficiently.

Traditional methods of publishing are no longer the only option for authors. Modern computer advances and print on demand companies enable creative and know-how independent publishers, such as A.L. Savvy Publications to offer exciting and dynamic publishing opportunities for authors. According to a study by Publishers Weekly, in 2011 there were 211,269 self-published titles released based on ISBN's. 45% of those books were fiction while 38% were non-fiction. E-books accounted for 41% of self-published units sold. It is clear to see by these statistics that every day hundreds, even thousands of people are becoming self-published authors.

A.L. Savvy Publications will be able to compete in this flourishing self-publishing industry. A.L. Savvy Publications will be a noteworthy independent publishing house and produce titles in a full spectrum of categories fiction, non-fiction, novels and eBooks. The company will publish hardcover, trade paperback and e-book formats. A.L. Savvy Publications will develop a "cultural" series of e-articles written by a myriad of authors of different backgrounds to share insight and cultivate learning and understanding of diversity. A.L. Savvy Publications will respond quickly to trends to put books in the hands of readers more quickly and help generate reader's excitement about the books they aspire to peruse.

A.L. Savvy Publications will grow and become one of the largest independent publishers in the world. The company will deliver a finished product that is professional and of the highest quality. Creativity will indeed be a major part in the selling appeal for this promising business. A.L. Savvy Publications will be able to compete at an aggressive price level. For the first two years, the company will be a very compact operation. An in-home establishment is contemplated for years one through four. Focus will be on keeping the overhead to a minimum. Alberta Lampkins will contract with **Ingram Spark** for printing and distribution, as well as distributing e-books on such websites as **Amazon.com** and **Barnes & Noble**. She will purchase a group of ISBN's from Bowker U.S. ISBN Agency and will send all her own self-published titles to the U.S. Copyright office. Alberta Lampkins will devote 50% of the time marketing by creating a website, newsletters, brochures and mailers. Alberta Lampkins strategy for the success of A.L. Savvy Publications is by developing speaking engagements and classes. Alberta Lampkins will join organizations such as **Small Publishers Association of North America**, **The Authors Guild** or the **Association of American Publishers**. She will also participate in conferences, volunteer for speaking opportunities and offer to teach workshops, provide consulting, attend local meetings and get out meeting and networking with other writers and self-publishers.

Alberta Lampkins will continue education in publishing by taking on-line courses and webinars offered by associations such as **Publishing Executive** or other reputable organizations. She will take classes that will boost her knowledge and position her to be successful in not just writing, but also in publishing. Alberta Lampkins will also subscribe to publications that keep her up to date with current publishing and writing industry news, such as **Writer's Digest**, the **Writer's Magazine** and **Publisher's weekly**.

A.L. Savvy Publications will thrive as Alberta Lampkins possess boundless energy and is dedicated to working long hours to assure the success of the company she so proudly represents. Alberta Lampkins has a driving ambition to see the business grow and prosper, yet she is cautious in her approach and her expectations are quite reasonable. For the first two years, Alberta Lampkins will perform all the work, cover designs, editing, sales and production. By year three, the business will add on a full-time professional editor and a polished graphic designer.

A.L. Savvy Publications will give its customers not only a great product, but a creative arts experience that is guaranteed to uplift, inspire and move them through the written word.

Mission Statement

A.L. Savvy Publications is committed to bringing inspiration, innovation and creativity to the independent publishing world by setting high standards of quality service to our authors and our readers. A.L. Savvy Publications mission is to provide intriguing literature and cultivate a royal readership and reach out to authors looking for a smooth self-publishing experience.

A.L. Savvy Publications will create a publishing industry that celebrates authors and artists of all cultures and genres. In time, A. L. Savvy Publications will establish itself as the foremost independent publisher in the world of print.

Keys to Success

As A. L. Savvy Publications move towards the goal of being a world class independent publishing company, the business will follow these seven core values and guiding principles:

(1.) **Service Excellence** – giving the best service and achieving excellence each passing day.

(2.) **Ownership** – taking ownership of the business and customer success.

(3.) **Quality** – giving the best and unmatched results for all around satisfaction.

(4.) **Respect** – giving the respect due to self, our authors and our readers

(5.) **Innovation** – to come out with new, creative ideas that foster a greater propensity of success.

(6.) **Diversity** – respecting diversity and giving the best to the uniqueness of all authors, reader and all people in general.

(7.) **Community** – having a sense of responsibility and contributing to an abundant society of readers, authors and all others.

Objective

A.L. Savvy Publications primary goals over the next six-months are:

(1.) Secure a Small Business loan through the SBA for start-up of at least $5,000.

(2.) Set up files and office organization for business.

(3.) Acquire a group of ISBN's from Bowker U.S. ISBN Agency.

(4.) Set-up an Account for Print on Demand and distribution with Ingram Spark.

(5.) Create and design a website for A.L. Savvy Publications.

(6.) Finalize the editing, cover designs and copyrights for first four books that will be published by A.L. Savvy Publications.

(7.) Purchase business supplies, such as, event signage, paper stock for business cards, letterhead, shipping labels, mailers, envelopes and stationary.

(8.) Obtain a tax Identification number.

(9.) Join various publishing, small business and writer's associations.

(10.) Take on-line classes to help educate and/or teach to enhance knowledge of independent publishing and small business venture.

(11.) Launch A.L. Savvy Publications!

Description of Business

A.L. Savvy Publications was established in 2014 with the desire to publish a line of literary titles which support and cultivate new and established authors. In the sheer spirit of optimism and a good sense of business savvy, the company is dedicated to bringing those writers worthy of publication to an eager and geared up reading community.

A.L. Savvy Publications confidently established itself as a publisher of progressive and contemporary literature with a distinctly cultural sensibility. A.L. Savvy Publications is on its way to becoming known for its excellence in books and forward-thinking literary works. With local, national and global vision in mind, A.L. Savvy

Publications is firmly rooted in producing notable literary works.

A.L. Savvy Publications philosophy is, to be recognized as:

"A **S**ophisticated **and V**ery **V**ersatile company **Y**earning to turn out amazing **P**ublications"

The Company – Present Situation

A.L. Savvy Publications is in the final planning stages and is targeting a June 1, 2014 launch. A.L. Savvy Publications will launch print advertising, World Wide Web and social media advertising, distribute attractive fliers and host an intensive marketing sales campaign. A.L. Savvy Publications will be addressing a variety of markets. Unpublished authors and book clubs will represent two markets. The company will target a community of loyal readers that will grow purely – and build a solid readership base with each book release.

Company Ownership/Legal Entity

A.L. Savvy Publications is a completely owner-operated business, with Alberta Lampkins doing all the exertion. She is fully responsible for developing and managing, production, composition, and proofreading, editing, graphic layout, typesetting, and sales and marketing.

Location

A.L. Savvy Publications is currently a home-based business. The company has a P.O. Box for mailing and business purposes.

Market Analysis – Customers/Market Strategies

The need for authors to get their work in the hands of readers has been well established. The must for creative publishing that is proficient, professional and valuable is essential. It is that market that A.L. Savvy Publications intends to nurture. Unpublished writers and readers make up the most fruitful domain in the spectrum of customers of independent publishers. The small medley of independent publishers doing business in Clarksville, TN lacks the presence of a diverse market. Alberta Lampkins will escalate that market through personal phone calls, business contacts each week and effective, creative printed and electronic marketing material. Alberta Lampkins will demonstrate to her writers and authors just how they can have a more appealing presence in the self-publishing world as a result of the skill and creativity of A.L. Savvy Publications.

Risks
Risks that are intrinsic to all businesses have been studied by Alberta Lampkins in the formation of the plan for A.L. Savvy Publications. There are no subsequent concerns regarding availability of books which will be produced primarily electronic and by print on demand services. The foremost risk is inability to reach a wide array of authors and readers and a chance of having unmarketable books. Other potential variations in the economy have been carefully evaluated by Alberta Lampkins. During economic downturns, far-sighted businesses not only

watch their cost more intently, but initiate sales-generating promotions through direct mail, electronic advertising and other print campaigns. A.L. Savvy Publications stands ready to fulfill the need and at an pleasing and even discounted price if warranted.

Diversity of author and reader base is strength of A.L. Savvy Publications because the company will be selling a wide range of fiction, non-fiction, novels and eBooks. Alberta Lampkins is largely reliant on the very dependable Print on Demand Company and distribution, therefore adding another dimension of might grounded on the diversification of the market.

Sample Press Release

FOR IMMEDIATE RELEASE
CONTACT: Alberta Lampkins
Email: albertalampkins@gmail.com
931-xxx-xxx (Business Cell)

BUFFALO NATIVE LAUNCHES HER DEBUT NOVEL

"Settle down and take a ride into a heartrending story of faith, friendship and forgiveness in Buffalo, New York, where snow covered trees aren't the only things icy in the hearts and lives of two neighborhood women."

BUFFALO, NEW YORK, June 27— a captivating new author will debut her novel *"Teach Me How to Fly"* July 5, 2014 as part of A.L. Savvy Publications line. She is planning an "It's a Savvy Affair" book launch party on July 5, 2014 at the Double Tree Club by Hilton Hotel Downtown Buffalo, 125 High Street. She will also promote the book *"Messages to Our Children,"* in which she is the Project Coordinator and contributing author.

Alberta, a proud Army wife and founder of A.L. Savvy Publications, has been working toward publication for more than five years while working as an Adult Services and Child

Protective Services Social Worker. In addition, she completed her Master of Arts Degree in Sociology from Fayetteville State University in 2012. Her graduate research project on HIV testing among African American women is accepted for scholarly publication in the *Journal of Research on Women and Gender,* Texas State University. All roads have led Alberta to following her dream of writing and publishing her first novel.

Set out on a train ride from Buffalo, New York headed to Virginia, *"Teach Me How to Fly"* is a contemporary story of Jocelyn Hamilton, wife of a retired Army Sergeant Major and coffee shop owner in Buffalo, New York, who receives a strange phone call after the death of her mother. The phone call strikes questions about her mother's past. Jocelyn is curious and determined to uncover the mystery, so she travels back to her mother's hometown of Martinsville, Virginia to meet the one lady who can give her the answers she wants. However, while Jocelyn is busy putting the pieces of her mother's past together, her friend Angel Medina, a fashion designer working downtown in Buffalo, is desperately seeking to keep her long-ago life tucked away. Angel soon comes face to face with the one person she hoped she would never see again. What happens to a broken soul left untreated? Can you really escape what lies behind you? How do you learn to forgive? Jocelyn and Angel find strength through their unexpected friendship in *Teach Me How to Fly*.

Alberta Lampkins insightful debut novel has it all and takes the readers on a heart touching ride. It's a triumphant story about faith, friendship and forgiveness.

Alberta is available for interviews and appearances. For booking presentations, media appearances, interviews, and/or book-signings contact albertalampkins@gmail.com or call her at 931-xxx-xxx. Visit her on the web at http://alsavvypublications.com.
Facebook.com/ALSavvyPublications or Twitter.com/ALSavvyPub.

ALBERTA LAMPKINS

DESCRIPTIVE WORDS

Feelings beginning with A:
Angry, annoyed, agreeable, afraid, awkward, affectionate, anxious, alarmed. Awful, abandoned, absent minded, accepted, aggravated

Feelings beginning with B:
Brave, bored, bothered, bewildered, brilliant, bitter, bashful, bad, blue, baffled, bummed out

Feelings beginning with C:
Confused, cheery, cooperative, caring, confident, calm, clumsy, curious, content, competent, compassionate, considerate, cautious, cranky, clever

Feelings beginning with D:
Disorganized, defiant, depressed, discouraged, delighted, disgusted, determined, disappointed, dumb, detached, destructive, daring, disillusioned, devious

Feelings beginning with E:
Energetic, encouraged, enthusiastic, embarrassed, edgy, excited, empathetic, envious, exhausted, eager, exuberant, expectant, enraged

Feelings beginning with F:
Friendly, funny, frightened, fearful, furious, foolish, fed up, frustrated, forgiving, flustered, fortunate

Feelings beginning with G:
Grouchy, guilty, great, groovy, grief-stricken, generous, greedy, grateful, gullible, grumpy, green with envy

Feelings beginning with H:
Happy, humiliated, hurt, helpless, hopeless, honest, horrified, hesitant, hilarious, humble, honored, heartbroken

Feelings beginning with I:
Irritated, interested, insecure, impatient, ignored, inspired, inadequate, irrational, ignorant, indifferent, irked, irresponsible, invisible

Feelings beginning with J:
Jealous, joyful, judgmental, jumpy, jaded, jocular, jinxed

Feelings beginning with K:
Kind, keen, knocked down, kooky,

Feelings beginning with L:
Laid back, loving, lonely, labile, lackluster, light-hearted, likeable, lost, lousy, lucky, lazy, loopy, leery

Feelings beginning with M:
Mad, mixed-up, meek, mean, miserable, malevolent, marvelous, magical, manipulated, manipulative, maternal, modest, misunderstood, mischievous, mopey, mistrustful, mellow, melodramatic, and moody

Feelings beginning with N:

Nice, naughty, nasty, nauseated, nervous, nerdy, nutty, noble, noisy, neglected, neglectful, needy, needed, nifty, naive, nonchalant, nonplussed

Feelings beginning with O:

Okay, overpowered, overjoyed, over-the-top, obedient, obsessive, off, odd, offended, out-of-control, outraged, overloaded, overstimulated, obstinate, obligated

Feelings beginning with P:

Panicked, peaceful, playful, pensive, proud, peeved, patronized, peachy, perfect, peppy, pensive, puzzled, powerful, powerless, picky, pleased, psyched, petty, petulant, preoccupied

Feelings beginning with Q:

Quiet, questioned, questionable, quirky, quarrelsome, quivery, qualified, querulous

Feelings beginning with R:

Respected, relieved, relaxed, resentful, rattled, refreshed, repulsed, rageful, rational, reasonable, reactive, ready, rebellious, reluctant, reassured, restive, restful, remorseful, reserved

Feelings beginning with S:

Sad, surprised, silly, smiley, scared, sorry, serious, stupid, shy, satisfied, sensitive, safe, stressed out, stubborn, sarcastic, sassy, spiteful, scornful, secure, serene, smug, snarky, snarly, sociable

Feelings beginning with T:

Thankful, tearful, thoughtful, terrific, talkative, tolerant, trusted, temperamental, terrified, timid, tired, tantrum, troubled, tickled, torn, trustworthy, touched, threatened

Feelings beginning with U:

Understood, understanding, uneasy, uncertain, ugly, uncomfortable, unruffled, unafraid, useless, unimpressed, unappreciated, undecided, unique, unruly, up

Feelings beginning with V:

Vivacious, vain, vibrant, violent, valued, vital, vexed, volatile, vulnerable, victorious, vacant

Feelings beginning with W:

Worried, wacky, wary, weak, weary, weird, wistful, woeful, weepy, well, whiny, worn out, wound up, whimsical, warm, witty, withdrawn, worthless, wronged, willful, wishful

Feelings beginning with X:

Xenophobic, X'd out

Feelings beginning with Y:

Yucky, yappy, youthful, yielding, yearning

Feelings beginning with Z:

Zany, zealous, zonked, zippy, zestful, Zen, zapped

Words used to describe clothing

A-line

an A-line skirt fits closely around the waist and is slightly wider at the bottom

Backless

a backless dress does not cover a woman's back and shoulders

Baggy

baggy clothes are very loose on your body

Best

used for referring to your nicest or most expensive clothes that you wear on special occasions

Boot-cut

boot-cut trousers become slightly wider at the bottom so that they fit easily over boots

Brief

Not covering much of your body

Button-down

a button-down shirt has the ends of the collar fastened to the shirt with buttons

Button-through

a button-through skirt or dress has buttons that go from the top to the bottom

Casual

casual clothes are comfortable, and suitable for wearing in informal situations

Clingy
fitting in a way that shows the shape of your body
Close-fitting
Showing the shape of your body
Comfortable
Pleasant to wear, hold, or use
Conservative
conservative clothing or styles are traditional and without decoration
Cool
cool clothes prevent you from feeling too hot
Décolleté
a piece of woman's clothing that is décolleté is very low at the top so that you can see part of her shoulders and breasts
Designer
designer clothes are made by a famous designer and are usually expensive and fashionable
Double-breasted
a double-breasted jacket or coat has two parallel lines of buttons down the front when it is fastened
Dressy
dressy clothes are worn on formal occasions
Drip-dry
Drip-dry clothes do not need ironing
Easy-care

easy-care clothes do not need to be ironed after they are washed

-fitting

used with some adjectives and adverbs to make adjectives describing how clothing fits someone

Flame-retardant

flame-retardant clothing or substances have been treated with chemicals that stop them from burning easily in a fire

Formal

formal clothes are the special clothes that people wear at formal occasions, usually a black jacket and trousers for men and a long dress for women

Full

a full piece of clothing is loose on your body because it contains a lot of cloth

Full-length

a full-length coat, dress, or skirt goes down to your feet

Full-length

a full-length sleeve goes to your wrist

Hard-wearing

hard-wearing clothing is strong and lasts a long time

Heavy

heavy clothes, shoes, or materials are thick and strong

Homespun

homespun clothes are made from cloth that someone has produced at home
Hooded
With a hood
Hooded
wearing a piece of clothing that has a hood
Ill-fitting
ill-fitting clothes are the wrong size for the person wearing them
Informal
used about the type of clothes that you wear at home or to relax
Itchy
used about clothes that make you feel like this
Jackie-O
fashionable in the style of Jacqueline Onassis
Knee-length
Reaching your knees
Light
light clothes are made of thin cloth and are not very warm
Lined
clothing that is lined has another layer of cloth on the inside
Long
long dresses, trousers, sleeves etc. cover your arms or

legs

Loose

loose clothes are large and do not fit your body tightly

Loose-fitting

loose-fitting clothes are large, comfortable, and not tight

Low

a piece of clothing that is low shows your neck and a lot of your chest

Low-cut

a low-cut dress or blouse shows a woman's chest and the top part of her breasts because it has a low neckline

Machine washable

able to be washed in a washing machine without being damaged

Made-to-measure

Made to fit a particular person. Clothes that have not been made for a particular person are ready-to-wear or off-the-peg.

Modest

modest behavior or clothes are intended to avoid causing sexual feelings in other people: used mainly about women

Non-iron

non-iron clothes do not need to be ironed (=made

smooth) after they have been washed

Off-the-peg

off-the-peg clothes are not made to fit a particular person

Off-the-rack

Off-the-peg

One-piece

consisting of one piece of clothing, or made from one piece of material, rather than separate parts

Open-necked

an open-necked shirt is a shirt whose top button is not fastened

Oversized

used about clothes that are designed to look large

Padded

padded clothes are filled with a soft substance to protect or change the appearance of your body

Peaked

a peaked cap or hat has a flat curved part that continues beyond the main part at the front above the eyes

Plunging

a plunging neckline or dress shows a lot of the top part of a woman's breasts

Preshrunk

preshrunk clothes do not get smaller when you wash

them because the cloth was shrunk before the clothes were made

Prim

prim clothes are neat, sensible, and show very little of your body

Prissy

prissy clothes or designs look silly because they are too tidy and traditional

Raglan

a raglan sleeve goes right up to your neck, without a separate join at the shoulder

Raglan

used about a piece of clothing with raglan sleeves

Rainproof

rainproof material or clothing prevents rain from passing through it

Ready-to-wear

Ready-to-wear clothes are ready-made

Revealing

showing a part of someone's body that is usually covered

Reversible

able to be used or worn on both sides

Rolled-up

rolled-up sleeves or trousers have their ends folded

over several times to make them shorter

Roomy

roomy clothing is large and comfortable

Rushed

rushed clothes or curtains are made with many small folds pulled close together

Sartorial

relating to clothes or to how they are made

Scanty

scanty clothes show parts of your body that are usually covered

Seamed

Made with a seam

Seamless

Made without seams

Sensible

sensible clothes or shoes are practical and comfortable rather than fashionable

Showerproof

showerproof coats and jackets keep you dry in light rain but not in heavy rain

Single-breasted

a single-breasted jacket has one row of buttons

Skimpy

skimpy clothes fit very tightly and do not cover very much of someone's body. This word often shows that you do not approve of clothes like this

Skinny

skinny clothes fit your body very tightly

Skin-tight

skin-tight clothes fit your body very tightly

Sleeveless

a sleeveless dress or shirt is one that does not have sleeves

Slimming

making you look thinner than you really are

Sloppy

sloppy clothes are loose and informal

Smart

Used about someone's clothes

Snug

fitting closely to your body, or fitting closely into a space

Sporty

sporty clothes are designed to be worn for sport or on informal occasions

Starched

starched clothes have been made stiff with starch

Straight

a straight skirt, pair of trousers etc. hangs down close to your body

Strapless

without straps that go over your shoulders

Strappy
strappy clothes or shoes have several straps

Stretch
stretch cloth or clothing becomes wider or longer when you pull it and returns to its original shape and size when you stop pulling it

Stretchy
stretchy cloth or clothing can be stretched and will go back to its original shape

Tailored
tailored clothes are shaped in a way that matches the shape of a person's body

Tailor-made
tailor-made clothes are made by a tailor to fit a particular customer

Thermal
thermal clothing is made of special material that keeps you warm

Threadbare
threadbare clothing, carpet, or cloth is very thin and almost has holes in it because it has been worn or used a lot

Tight
clothes that are tight are close against your body when

you wear them
Tight-fitting
Fitting very tightly
Two-piece
consisting of two matching pieces of clothing, one for the top part of your body and one for the bottom part
Underwired
an underwired bra has two curved metal wires sewn into it that support a woman's breasts
Unfashionable
used for describing clothes like this
Unlined
unlined curtains or clothing have no lining (=extra layer of cloth) on the inside
Voluminous
voluminous clothing has a lot of material in it and is loose on your body
-waisted
used with some adjectives to make other adjectives describing the type of waist that a person or piece of clothing has
Washable
able to be washed without being damaged
Waterproof
waterproof clothes keep you dry because they do not let rain pass through them

Wearable

wearable clothes are comfortable and easy to wear

Weatherproof

Providing protection from bad weather

Wraparound

wrapped around your body and tied rather than being fastened with buttons etc.

Zip-up

Closed by means of a zip

Monogrammed

Pleated

Polo-neck

V-necked

Down to

used for saying how long someone's hair is or how long their clothes are

Words used to describe a person's general shape

Barrel-chested

a man who is barrel-chested has a large chest that curves outwards

Beefy

a beefy person has a large heavy body and strong muscles

Big

a big person is tall and heavy, and often fat

Brawny

Physically strong, with big muscles

Built

used for describing the size and shape of someone's body

Bullnecked

With a short thick neck

Burly

a burly man is fat and strong

Coltish

tall and thin, and tending to move fast

Compact

a compact person is physically small but looks strong

Full

if part of someone's body is full, it is large, wide, or has a round shape, especially in a way that is attractive

Gangling

very tall and thin, with long arms and legs, and not graceful

Gangly

Gangling

Gawky

tall and thin, and moving in a way that does not seem graceful or comfortable

Heavy-set

Big and strong

Herculean

a herculean person is very big and strong

Husky

a husky boy or man is big and strong

Lank

a lank person is tall and thin

Lanky

Tall, thin, and not very graceful

Leggy

a leggy woman has long attractive legs

Musclebound

someone who is musclebound has extremely large strong muscles as a result of too much exercise

Muscular

very strong and attractive, with muscles that have been developed through exercise

Paunchy

With a paunch

Pear-shaped

a pear-shaped person is larger below the waist than above the waist

Pigeon-chested

someone who is pigeon-chested has a chest that sticks out in an unusual way

Round-shouldered

with shoulders that are bent forward

Slight

thin, not very tall, and not looking very strong

Slightly-built

someone who is slightly-built is thin, not very tall, and does not look very strong

Solid

someone who looks solid is big and has a strong firm body

Statuesque

Tall and beautiful like a statue

Stocky

a stocky person looks strong but is not tall

Stooped

Stooping

Trapping

Tall and strong

Taut

a taut body is firm with strong muscles and little fat

Thickset

someone who is thickset has a wide strong body

Well-built

a well-built person has a body that people admire because of its strength or beauty

Willowy

Tall, thin, and graceful

Burliness

Gawkiness

Lankiness

An hourglass figure

the shape of a woman's body if she has a small waist and large breasts and hips

A wisp of a...

A small and delicate person

Be built like a brick shithouse

To be very big and strong

Heavily built

a heavily built person is big and strong but not fat

Words to describe someone's facial features

Baby-faced

a baby-faced adult has a round face like a young child's

Chiseled

An American spelling of chiseled

Chiseled

a man who has a chiseled face, mouth etc. has a face, mouth etc. that looks very strong and is regular in size and shape

Craggy

a craggy face looks strong and has deep lines in it

Fine

if someone has fine features, their eyes, nose, etc. look small and delicate

Fresh-faced

healthy and with a face that looks young

Full-face

showing all of someone's face looking straight at you

Furrowed

Covered with deep lines

Good-looking

physically attractive, especially with an attractive face

Handsome

a handsome man or boy has a very attractive face

Handsome

a handsome woman has an attractive face with strong and regular features

Hatchet-faced

having a long, thin, and unpleasant looking face with a pointed nose and chin

Lived-in

someone who has a lived-in face is quite old, but looks as if they have had an interesting life

Made-up

Wearing make-up on your face

Sculpted

a part of someone's face or body that is sculpted is very firm or straight in an attractive way

Seamed
a seamed face has a lot of lines in the skin
Snub-nosed
with a short nose that looks rather flat
Thin
someone with thin features has a long narrow mouth, nose etc.
Unlined
an unlined face shows no signs of old age
Weak
a weak part of a person's face is one that is small and suggests a poor character
Weather-beaten
a weather-beaten face has rough skin from being outside for long periods

Words to describe someone's hair
Bad hair day
a day when your hair looks untidy and you do not feel attractive

Bald
with little or no hair on your head
Balding
Beginning to lose your hair
Body

a thick healthy appearance of your hair

Bouffant

bouffant hair is arranged in a style that lifts it away from your head

Bristly

Bristly hair is short and rough

Bushy

bushy hair or fur is very thick

Close-cropped

Cut very short

Coiffed

coiffed hair has been carefully arranged in a special style

Coiffured

coiffured hair has been carefully arranged in a special style

Crinkly

Crinkly hair is rough and curly

Curl

the way that someone's hair grows in curls

Disheveled

An American spelling of disheveled

Disheveled

if you are disheveled, your hair and clothes do not look tidy

Flowing

flowing clothes or hair hang in an attractive way

Flyaway

flyaway hair is very thin and soft, so that it is difficult to keep in a tidy hairstyle

Frizz

the condition of hair that has very small tight stiff curls

Frizzy

frizzy hair has small tight stiff curls

Fuzzy

covered with short soft hairs or fibers like hair

Gloss

the shiny and attractive appearance of something, especially someone's hair

Hairless

With no hair

Hairy

With a lot of hair

Lank

Lank hair is thin and straight

Loose

if your hair is loose, it is not tied in position

Luxuriant

Luxuriant hair is thick and healthy

Matted

matted hair or fur is twisted or stuck together and

usually dirty

Nappy

nappy hair is tightly curled or twisted. This word is used especially by black people.

Scraggly

scraggly hair is untidy and does not look clean or healthy

Shaggy

Long, thick, and untidy

Shoulder-length

shoulder-length hair reaches down to your shoulders

Saphead

an insulting way of referring to a man who is bald

Sleek

sleek fur or hair is smooth and shiny

Spiky

Spiky hair sticks up

Split ends

a condition in which the ends of your hair are split into two or more parts

Straight

straight hair has no curls or waves

Swept-back

swept-back hair is brushed away from your forehead

Thick

thick hair or fur is made of many small hairs growing very close together

Thin

thin hair, fur, or plants do not look solid because there are spaces between the individual hairs or leaves

Tidy

tidy hair, clothes etc. look good because they are arranged in a nice way

Tousled

tousled hair looks untidy in an attractive way

Unkempt

Dirty and untidy

Wavy

a wavy line or wavy hair has a lot of waves or curls in it

Wind-blown

looking untidy because of being blown around by the wind

Windswept

someone who is windswept looks untidy because their clothes and hair have been blown around by a strong wind

Wiry

wiry hair or grass is stiff and rough

Blow-dried

Braided

Fuzziness

Lankly

Lankness

Luxuriantly

Shagginess

Tonsured

Waviness

Down to

used for saying how long someone's hair is or how long their clothes are

Thin on top

Losing your hair

Words to describe someone's walk

Sure-footed

good at walking or climbing and unlikely to fall

Springy

if you walk with a springy step, you walk quickly and with a lot of energy

Rolling

someone who has a rolling walk moves their body from side to side as they walk

Footing

a firm position for your feet on a surface, especially one that is difficult to stand on or walk across

In/into step

if people walk in step, each person moves their feet at exactly the same time as the others

Out of step

if people walk out of step, they do not keep their feet moving at the same time as the rest of a group

On foot

Walking

Lumbering

walking slowly because of being large and heavy

Words to describe someone's speech style

Articulate

able to express your thoughts, arguments, and ideas clearly and effectively

Articulate

articulate writing or speech is clear and easy to understand

Chatty

a chatty writing style is friendly and informal

Circuitous

taking a long time to say what you really mean when you are talking or writing about something

Clean

clean language or humor does not offend people, especially because it does not involve sex

Conversational

a conversational style of writing or speaking is informal, like a private conversation

Crisp

crisp speech or writing is clear and effective

Declamatory

expressing feelings or opinions with great force

Diffuse

using too many words and not easy to understand

Discursive

including information that is not relevant to the main subject

Economical

an economical way of speaking or writing does not use more words than are necessary

Elliptical

suggesting what you mean rather than saying or writing it clearly

Eloquent

expressing what you mean using clear and effective language

Emphatic

making your meaning very clear because you have very strong feelings about a situation or subject

Emphatically

Very firmly and clearly

Epigrammatic
expressing something such as a feeling or idea in a short and clever or funny way

Epistolary
Relating to the writing of letters

Euphemistic
euphemistic expressions are used for talking about unpleasant or embarrassing subjects without mentioning the things themselves

Flowery
flowery language or writing uses many complicated words that are intended to make it more attractive

Fluent
expressing yourself in a clear and confident way, without seeming to make an effort

Formal
correct or conservative in style, and suitable for official or serious situations or occasions

Gossipy
a gossipy letter is lively and full of news about the writer of the letter and about other people

Grandiloquent
expressed in extremely formal language in order to impress people, and often sounding silly because of this

Idiomatic

expressing things in a way that sounds natural

In

using a particular type or style of writing

Inarticulate

not able to express clearly what you want to say

Inarticulate

Not spoken or pronounced clearly

Incoherent

Unable to express yourself clearly

Informal

used about language or behavior that is suitable for using with friends but not in formal situations

Journalistic

Similar in style to journalism

Learned

a learned piece of writing shows great knowledge about a subject, especially an academic subject

Literary

involving books or the activity of writing, reading, or studying books

Literary

relating to the kind of words that are used only in stories or poems, and not in normal writing or speech

Lyric

using words to express feelings in the way that a song would

Lyrical
Having the qualities of music

Ornate
using unusual words and complicated sentences

Orotund
containing extremely formal and complicated language intended to impress people

Parenthetical
not directly connected with what you are saying or writing

Pejorative
a pejorative word, phrase etc. expresses criticism or a bad opinion of someone or something

Picturesque
picturesque language is unusual and interesting

Pithy
a pithy statement or piece of writing is short and very effective

Poetic
expressing ideas in a very sensitive way and with great beauty or imagination

Polemical
using or supported by strong arguments

Ponderous

ponderous writing or speech is serious and boring

Portentous

trying to seem very serious and important, in order to impress people

Prolix

using too many words and therefore boring

Punchy

a punchy piece of writing such as a speech, report, or slogan is one that has a strong effect because it uses clear simple language and not many words

Rambling

a rambling speech or piece of writing is long and confusing

Readable

writing that is readable is clear and able to be read

Rhetorical

relating to a style of speaking or writing that is effective or intended to influence people

Rhetorical

written or spoken in a way that is impressive but is not honest

Rhetorically

in a way that expects or wants no answer

Rhetorically

Using or relating to rhetoric

Rough

a rough drawing or piece of writing is not completely finished

Roundly

In a strong and clear way

Sententious

expressing opinions about right and wrong behavior in a way that is intended to impress people

Sesquipedalian

using a lot of long words that most people do not understand

Shakespearean

using words in the way that is typical of Shakespeare's writing

Slangy

containing or using a lot of slang

Stylistic

relating to ways of creating effects, especially in language and literature

Succinct

expressed in a very short but clear way

Turgid

using language in a way that is complicated and difficult to understand

Unprintable

used for describing writing or words that you think are offensive

Vague
someone who is vague does not clearly or fully explain something

Vaguely
in a way that is not clear

Verbose
using more words than necessary, and therefore long and boring

Well-turned
a well-turned phrase is one that is expressed well

Worded
Expressed in a particular way

Wordy
using more words than are necessary, especially long or formal words

Articulately

Circuitously

Circumlocutory

Conversationally

Eloquently

Euphemistically

Fluently

Idiomatically

Inarticulately

Incoherently

Lyrically

Parenthetically
Pejoratively
Pithily
Pleonastic

Ponderously
Portentously
Sensationalist
Stylistically
Succinctly
Be couched in something
To be expressed a particular way
Have something/a lot/nothing etc. to say for yourself
to be fairly/very/not at all keen to talk, especially about yourself and your reasons for doing something
With (your) tongue in (your) cheek

Descriptive words for Hair?

A Cascade Of Curls, Afro, Airy, Auburn, Balding, Bangs, Barrett, Beautiful, Beehive, Big Hair, Black, Bleached, Blonde, Blow Dry, Bob, Bobby Pins, Bonnet, Bouffant, Bouncy, Bowl Cut, Braids, Bright, Brown, Brunette, Brushed, Bun, Busby, Bushy, Buzz Cut, Cap, Carrot Top,

Chestnut, Chignon, Chocolate, Choppy, Cinnamon, Clasps, Clips, Coiffure, Comb Over, Combs, Copper, Copper Red, Corkscrews, Cornrows, Coronet, Course, Cowlick, Crew Cut, Crimped, Crimper, Cropped, Crown, Curlers, Curling Iron, Curls, Curly, Dandruff, Dark, Dark Chocolate, Diffuser, Dirty, Dirty Blond, Dirty Blonde, Do, Downy, Dreadlocks, Ducktail, Dulled Gold, Dyed, Ebony, Fair, Fair-Haired, Fall, Faux-Hawk, Feathered, Fiery, Finger Wave, Flame Like, Flaming Red, Flattop, Flaxen, Flip, Flowing, Flowy, Follicle, Forelock, French Knot, French Twist, Fringe, Frizzy, Frosted, Fuzzy, Gel, Glisten, Glossy, Glowing, Golden, Golden Butterscotch, Gorgeous, Gossamer, Greasy, Grey, Groomed, Hairdo, Hair Extensions, Hairpiece, Hairpins, Hairspray, Hanging, Hard To Manage, Hat, Hat-Hair, Headband, Helmet, Highlights, Hi-Top, Honey Blond, Honey Blonde, Hood, Jet Black, Jheri Curl, Kinky, Knotted, Lackluster, Layered, Lock, Long, Loose, Luscious, Lustrous, Mane, Messy, Miter, Mohawk, Mop, Mousse, Mud Gutter Blond, Mud Like, Mullet, Nap, Nappy, Oily, Onyx, Out Of Control, Pageboy, Pale Champagne, Part,

Peach Fuzz, Pecan Blond, Permanent, Permed, Pigtails, Pin Straight, Pixie, Plait, Platinum, Pomade, Pompadour, Ponytail, Pretty, Puffed, Radiant, Rattail, Ratty, Raven, Razor Cut, Red, Redhead, Ribbons, Ringlets, Rubber Bands, Sable, Sandy, Scrunched, Scrunchies, Shag, Shaggy, Shampoo, Shape, Shaved, Shimmering, Shiny, Shiny, Short, Shoulder Length, Sideburns, Silken Blonde, Silky, Silver, Skinhead, Sleek, Slick, Smarmy, Soft, Spiked, Spikes, Spirals, Split Ends, Spray, Straggly, Straight, Strand, Strawberry Blond, Streak, Stringy, Stripped, Stubbly, Style, Sun Streaked, Tangled, Tasseled, Tawny, Teased, Tendrils, Texture, Thick, Thinning, Tiara, Tinted, Titian, Toque, Toupe, Tousled, Towhead, Tress, Trim, Turban, Unkempt, Upswept, Wavy, Weave, Widow Peak, Wig, Wild, Windblown, Windswept, Wings, Wiry, Wispy, Wooly, Yellow.

Descriptive words for Texture?

Abrasive, Acute, Angular, Arid, Ballooned, Bendable, Biting, Blemished, Blistered, Boiling, Bouncy, Bristly, Broad, Bubbly, Bulging, Bumpy,

Burning, Burnished, Bushy, Caked, Caressing, Carved, Chafing, Channeled, Chapped, Cheap, Cheerful, Chunky, Clammy, Clean, Clear, Coagulated, Coarse, Coating, Cold, Concentrated, Confused, Cool, Copious, Corduroy, Corrugated, Cottony, Covering, Cratered, Crawly, Creamy, Creepy, Crocheted, Crude, Crumbly, Curdled, Cushioned, Cut, Cutting, Damaged, Damp, Dank, Decorated, Deep, Defective, Definite, Dehydrated, Dense, Dented, Difficult, Dirty, Discoloration, Disfigured, Distended, Downy, Dreary, Drenched, Dripping, Dry, Ductile, Dull, Durable, Dusty, Effective, Elastic, Emblazoned, Embossed, Enameled, Encrusted, Engraved, Enlarged, Etched, Even, Expanded, Feathery, Fiery, Filmy, Filthy, Fine, Firm, Flattened, Flawless, Fleecy, Fluted, Foamy, Freezing, Fresh, Frigid, Frothy, Furry, Fuzzy, Glassy, Glazed, Glossy, Glutinous, Gooey, Grainy, Granular, Grating, Gravelly, Greasy , Grimy, Grinding, Gripped, Gritty, Grooved, Grubby, Grungy, Hairy, Hard, Hard , Harsh, Hatched, Hazy, Heated, Hoarse, Honeyed, Hot, Humid, Hygienic, Icy, Immaculate, Impenetrable, Imprinted, Incised,

Incisive, Indented, Inflated, Inflexible, Inlaid, Inscribed, Inviting, Ironed, Irregular, Itching, Ivory, Jagged, Jarring, Jumbled, Keen, Kiss, Knitted, Knobbed, Lacy, Layer, Level, Limp, Lined, Long-haired, Lustrous, Malleable, Marked, Matte, Matted, Metallic, Mild, Moist, Moist , Mosaic, Mucky, Mushy, Muted, Mutilated, Neat, Numbing, Orderly, Ornamented, Padded, Parched, Patina, Patterned, Perfect, Piercing, Pitted, Pleated, Pliable, Plush, Pocked, Pockmarked, Pointed, Pointy, Polished, Potholed, Precise, Pressed, Prickly, Printed, Protected, Pulpy, Pure, Ragged, Rasping, Raw, Refined, Reflective, Restful, Ribbed, Ridged, Rigid, Rocking, Rough, Runny, Rutted, Sandy, Sanitary, Satiny, Saturated, Scalding, Scaled, Scarred, Scorching, Scored, Scraped, Scratched, Scratching, Scratchy, Sculptured, Searing, Serrated, Set In, Severe, Shaggy, Sharp, Sharp-Edged, Sheen, Sheer, Shielded, Shiny, Shipshape, Silky, Skin, Sleek, Slick, Slight, Slimy, Slippery, Slovenly, Smooth, Smoothed, Smudged, Snarling, Snug, Soaked, Soaking, Soapy, Sodden, Soft, Soggy, Soiled, Solid,

Sopping, Sound, Sparkling, Spikey, Spiky, Spiny, Splintered, Spongy, Spotless, Springy, Squishy, Stain, Stamped, Steamed, Steely, Sterile, Sticky, Stiff, Still, Stinging, Stodgy, Strong, Stubbly, Stubbly, Substantial, Supported, Sweet, Sweltering, Swollen, Syrupy, Tangled, Tarnish, Tessellated, Thick, Thin, Thorny, Tickling, Tidy, Tiled, Tingly, Toothed, Tough, Translucent, Transparent, Tweedy, Unadulterated, Unblemished, Unbreakable, Unclear, Uncomfortable, Uncompromising, Unctuous, Understated, Undulation, Uneven, Unexciting, Uninteresting, Unpolluted, Unsoiled, Untainted, Untarnished, Untidy, Unyielding, Vague, Varnished, Velvety, Veneered, Very Cold, Viscous, Vivacious, Warm, Waterlogged, Wavy, Waxy, Waxy, Welcoming, Well-Defined, Well-Honed, Wet, Whetted, Wholesome, Wide, Withered, Wool, Woolly, Woven.

Descriptive words to describe Art?

Actual, Alluring, Ambiguous, Ambitious, Amorphous, Analytical, Angular, Asymmetrical, Audacious, Balanced, Beautiful, Blurred, Bold,

Brash, Bright, Broken, Bumpy, Calm, Captivating, Challenging, Clear, Closed, Coarse, Complementary, Contour, Contrasting, Controlled, Cool, Corrugated, Critical, Curvaceous, Curved, Dark, Deep, Diagonal, Distorted, Dramatic, Dull, Dusty, Elegant, Elongated, Elusive, Energetic, Exciting, Fine, Flat, Flowing, Foreground, Free Form, Freehand, Frenetic, Furry, Fuzzy, Garish, Geometric, Glorious, Glowing, Gooey, Grayed, Harsh, Heavy, Horizontal, Illusory, Imaginative, Implied, Interrupted, Isomorphic, Leathery, Light, Linear, Magnificent, Massive, Meandering, Medium, Meticulous, Middle ground, Monochromatic, Moving, Multicolored, Muted, Nebulous, Negative, Non-Conformist, Open, Organic, Pale, Patterned, Positive, Powerful, Prickly, Primary, Professional, Provocative, Rough, Ruled, Sandy, Saturated, Seamless, Secondary, Shallow, Shiny, Short, Simulated, Skilled, Smooth, Soft, Soothing, Sticky, Straight, Subdued, Subtle, Symmetrical, Tacky, Talented, Tertiary, Thick, Thin, Three Dimensional, Tinted, Triad, Two Dimensional, Uneven, Velvety, Vertical, Vibrant, Warm, Wet,

Wide.

Descriptive words for Chocolate?

addicted, aromatic, a sweet delight, a treat, baking chocolate, bar, bitter chocolate, bitter sweet, bitter sweet chocolate, brown, brownie, cacao, cafe, caffeine, candied, centre, choc, choc-ice, chocolate, chocolate bar, chocolate candy, chocolate chip cookie, chocolate syrup, coat, cocoa, cocoa bean, cocoa butter, cocoa powder, comforting, contentment, cures, dark chocolate, deep brown, delicious, delightful, desirable, enjoyable, fattening, fudge, hot chocolate, java, kiss, luscious, luxurious, melting moments, melts, milk chocolate, mocha, plain chocolate, powdered, rich, satisfying, sensual, smooth, soft, soothing, succulent, sweet, tantalizing, tiramisu, truffle, yummy .

Descriptive words for Beauty?

Here is a list of words that describe Beauty.

Total number of Beauty words and adjectives: 76 words

Beauty words are listed in alphabetical order.

Adorable, Alluring, Amazing, Appealing, Attractive, Awe-Inspiring, Beauteous, Beautiful, Blossom, Breathtaking, Brilliant, Charming, Comforting, Cover Girl, Cute, Dainty, Dazzling, Delicate, Delightful, Diva, Divine, Elegant, Engaging, Exquisite, Eye-Catching, Fair, Fetching, Flabbergasting, Flawless, Foxy, Friendly, Glamorous, Glorious, Good-Looking, Gorgeous, Graceful, Grand, Handsome, Heart-Filling, Heart-Warming, Horrible, Hot, Impressive, Incredible, Jaw-Dropping, Kind, Kindful, Loveliest, Loveliness, Lovely, Magnificent, Mystifying, Nice-Looking, Outstanding, Perfect, Pin-Up, Pleasant, Prepossessing, Pretty, Radiant, Ravishing, Resplendent, Sparkly, Spectacular, Splendid, Statuesque, Stunning, Stupid, Sublime, Superb, Sweet, Watery, Willful, Wonderful, Wondrous.

Descriptive words for the Ocean?

aqua, aquamarine, aquatic, Atlantic, beautiful, blue, brave, briny, calm, Caribbean, cerulean, cloud, continuous, crushing force, crystal clear, daring, deep, deep blue, depressed, dim, drifting boats, ever-changing, everlasting, fearful, frightening, immense, Indian, indirect, intimate, intrusively, limitless, loud waves, luscious waves, majestic, marine, miserable, mist, mysterious, naked, never-ending, oceanic, ominous, pacific, paradise, peaceful, playful, pure, relaxing, rippling, sad, salty, sapphire, seven seas, shameless, shifty, shimmering, soft waves, tranquil, unfaithful, unstable, wavy, wide, wondrous, wondrous blue .

What are some descriptive words for Animals?

Here is a list of words that describe Animals.

Total number of Animal words and adjectives: 72 words

Animal words are listed in alphabetical order.

Adorable, Aggressive, Agile, Beautiful, Bossy, Candid, Carnivorous, Clever, Cold, Cold-Blooded, Colorful, Cuddly, Curious, Cute, Dangerous, Deadly, Domestic, Dominant, Energetic, Fast, Feisty, Ferocious, Fierce, Fluffy, Friendly, Furry, Fuzzy, Grumpy, Hairy, Heavy, Herbivorous, Jealous, Large, Lazy, Loud, Lovable, Loving,

Malicious, Maternal, Mean, Messy, Nocturnal, Noisy, Nosy, Picky, Playful, Poisonous, Quick, Rough, Sassy, Scaly, Short, Shy, Slimy, Slow, Small, Smart, Smelly, Soft, Spikey, Stinky, Strong, Stubborn, Submissive, Tall, Tame, Tenacious, Territorial, Tiny, Vicious, Warm, Wild.

Descriptive words for Cars?
Ambulance, Auto, Automobile, Boxcar, Bus, Cab, Carriage, Coach, Compact, Convertible, Coupe, Cruiser, Drive, Flat, Hardtop, Hatchback, Limo, Limousine, Machine, Motor, Motorcar, Passenger Car, Racer, Ride, Roadster, Sedan, Sports Car, Station Wagon, Taxi, Tourer, Vehicle, Wagon.

Descriptive words for writing Movie reviews?
Absorbing, Average, Big-Budget, Bland, Bloody, Boring, Brilliant, Brutal, Charismatic, Charming, Clever, Clichéd, Comical, Confused, Dazzling, Disappointing, Disgusting, Distasteful, Dramatic, Dreadful, Dull, Enjoyable, Entertaining, Excellent, Exciting, Expensive, Fantasy, Fascinating, Fast-Moving, First-Rate, Flawed, Funny, Highly-Charged, Hilarious, Imaginative,

Incredibly Tiresome, Insightful, Inspirational, Intriguing, Juvenile, Lasting, Legendary, Low-Budget, Moronic, Oddball, Ordinary, Original, Outdated, Picaresque, Pleasant, Powerful, Predictable, Questionable, Ripping, Riveting, Romantic, Sad, Satirical, Second-Rate, Senseless, Sensitive, Sentimental, Silly, Slow, So Unoriginal, Static, Stupid, Surprising, Suspenseful, Tender, Third-Rate, Thought Provoking, Tired, Tragic, Trite, Uneven, Uninteresting, Unpretentious, Uplifting, Uproarious, Violent, Wacky, Weak.

List of Descriptive Words and Adjectives for Touch and Feel

Cold

Cool

Crisp

Damp

Dry

Dull

Elastic

Explode

Feathery

Firm

Fishy

Fleshy

Fragile

Furry

Fuzzy

Gritty

Hairy

Hard

Hot

Icy

Leathery

Lukewarm

Moist

Oily

Pebbly

Prickly

Pulpy

Rough

Rubbery

Sandy

Satiny

Sharp

Silky

Slimy

Slippery

Smooth

Soft

Spongy

Steamy

Sticky

Stuccoes

Tacky

Tender

Tepid

Textured

Thick

Thin

Tough

Velvety

Warm

Waxy

Wet

Wooly

List of Descriptive Words and Adjectives for Taste

Alkaline

Bitter

Bittersweet

Bland

Burnt

Buttery

Crisp

Fishy

Fruity

Gingery

Hearty

Hot

Mellow

Oily

Oily

Overripe

Peppery

Raw

Ripe

Salty

Sour

Spicy

Spoiled

Sugary

Sweet

Tangy medicinal

Tasteless

Unripe

Vinegary

List of Descriptive Words and Adjectives for Smell

Acidy

Acrid

Aromatic

Balmy

Briny

Burnt

Damp

Dank

Earthy

Fishy

Fragrant

Fresh

Gamy

Gaseous

Mildewed

Moldy

Musty

Perfumed

Piney

Pungent

Putrid

Rancid

Reek

Rotten

Savory

Scented

Sharp

Sickly

Sour

Spicy

Spoiled

Stagnant

Stench

Sweet

Tempting

List of Descriptive Words and Adjectives for Hearing (Soft Sounds).

Buzz

Chime

Clink

Crackle

Faint

Gurgle

Harmony (musical)

Hiss

Hum

Hush

Inaudible

Lilting

Melody

Murmur

Mute

Mutter

Patter

Peep

Purr

Rush

Rustle

Sigh

Snap

Speechless

Still

Swish

Tinkle

Twitter

Whir

Whisper

Zing

List of Descriptive Words and Adjectives for Hearing (Loud Sounds).

Bang

Bark

Bedlam

Blare

Bleat

Bluster

Boom

Brawl

Bray

Bump

Caterwaul

Clamor

Clap

Clash

Crash

Deafening

Din

Discord

Earsplitting

Grate

Hubbub

Jangle

Noise

Pandemonium

Piercing

Racket

Rage

Rasp

Raucous

Riot

Roar

Rowdy

Rumble

Scream

Screech

Shout

Slam

Smash

Squawk

Stamp

Stomp

Thud

Thump

Thunder

Tumult

Whine

Whistle

Yell

Describing Words for Spring Season

Abloom	Active	Airy	Alive	April Fool's Day
Awakening	Baby Animals	Barefoot	Baseball	Baseball Bat
Baseball Field	Baseball Player	Beautiful	Bee	Beehive
Bird	Birth	Bloom	Blooming	Blossom
Blossoming	Blue	Blue Skies	Born	Bouquet
Breeze	Breezy	Bright	Bud	Budding
Bulbs	Bunny	Butterfly	Buzzing	Calf
Caterpillar	Changing	Cheerful	Cheery	Cherries
Chick	Chirping	Clean	Cloudless	Clouds
Clover	Crisp	Crocus	Crops	Daffodil
Daisy	Darting	Delightful	Duckling	Dugout
Earth Day	Easter	Easter Basket	Easter Bunny	Easter Egg
Egg	Eggs	Enjoyable	Fair	Farmer
Fertile	Flourishing	Flower	Flower Pot	Flowers
Fluffy	Foal	Fragrant	Free	Freesia

Fresh	Galoshes	Garden	Gardener	Gardening
Gentle	Good Friday	Gosling	Grass	Grassy
Green	Grow	Growing	Happy	Hatch
hatching	Money	Hyacinth	Incredible	Iris
Joyful	June	Kid	Kite	Lamb
Life Cycle	Light	Lilac	Lovely	Lush
March	May	Melt	Melting	Mother's Day
Narcissus	Nest	New	Newborn	New Leaves
Outdoor	Pastel	Peaceful	Plant	Playing
Pleasant	Plow	Pollinate	Polliwog	Pollywog
Poppy	Puddle	Puddles	Rabbit	Rain
Rain Boots	Rainbow	Raincoat	Rainy	Rebirth
Refreshing	Rejuvenating	Relaxing	Renewing	Robin
Romping	Saint Patrick's Day	Scampering	Season	Seasonal
Seed	Shower	Showers	Singing	Sky Blue

Describing Words for Winter Season

Arctic	Balaclava	Bare	Barren	Below Zero
Beret	Biting	Bitter Cold	Black Ice	Blanket
Bleak	Blizzard	Blustery	Bobsled	Bobsledding
Boots	Bored	Brisk	Candle	Candy

				Cane
Cap	Card	Carol	Chill	Chilling
Chills	Chilly	Chimney	Christmas	Clear
Clouds	Cloudy	Coat	Cocoon	Cold
Cold Snap	Comforter	Cough	Cozy	Crackling
Crisp	Crunchy	Crystalline	Curling	Dark
December	Decorate	Decorations	Depressing	Desolate
Dismal	Dog Sled	Down Coat	Drafty	Dreary
Drenched	Duvet	Ear flap Hat	Earmuff	Eggnog
Evergreen	Extreme	February	Fire	Fireplace
Fireside	Firewood	Fishing Pole	Flannel	Fleece
Fleecy	Flu	Fluffy	Flurries	Fog
Foggy	Freeze	Freezing	Freezing Rain	Frigid
Frost	Frostbite	Frostbitten	Frosty	Frozen
Fruitcake	Furnace	Gale	Garland	Gift
Gingerbread	Gingerbread House	Gingerbread Woman	Glacial	Glacier
Gloves	Goal	Goalie	Gray	Gust
Gusty	Hail	Hailstone	Hypothermia	Hypodermic
Hanukkah	Harsh	Hat	Hazy	Heat
Heated	Heater	Hibernate	Hockey	Hockey Puck
Hockey Stick	Holiday	Ice	Hot Chocolate	Iceberg

Ice Cap	Ice Cold	Ice Crystal	Ice Dam	Ice Fishing
Ice Hockey	Ice-Kissed	Ice Rink	Ice Knee-Deep	Kwanza
Storm	Stock	Stuck Inside	Snowfall	Snowflake
Sparkling	Spiced	Sugarplum	Sunny	Sweater
Temperature	Thaw	Thermometer	Toasty	Toboggan
Tobogganing	Winter Clothes	Winter Holidays	Winter Sports	Wintertime

Describing Words for Summer Season

Abloom	Active	Air-Conditioned	Air Conditioner	Alive
August	Backpacking	Backyard	Balmy	Barbeque
Barefoot	Baseball	Baseball Diamond	Bathing Suit	Beach
Beautiful	Berries	Blazing	Blistering	Blistering
Boat	Boating	Boiling	Breeze	Breezy
Bright	Camp	Campground	Camping	Campsite
Canoeing	Cheerful	Clammy	Clear	Cloudless
Cool Off	Corn On The Cob	Daisy	Damp	Delightful
Diving	Dreamy	Driving	Ease	Easy

Endless	Fan	Fireworks	Fish	Fishing
Fishing Boat	Fishing Pole	Flip Flops	Flowers	Fourth of July
Fragrant	Free	Fresh	Fresh Fruit	Fresh Produce
Frisbee	Garden	Gardener	Gardening	Gardening Tools
Bikini	Grass	Green	Grill	Grilled
Growing	Hamburgers	Happy	Hazy	Heat
Heat Wave	Heavenly	Hiker	Hiking	Hiking Trail
Holiday	Hot	Humid	Humidity	Ice Cream
Ice Cream Truck	Independence Day	Jet Ski	Journey	July
July Fourth	June	Lake	Lazy	Leisurely
Lemonade	Light	Lightening	Lovely	Lush
Memorial Day	Moist	Muggy	Natural	Ocean
Oppressive	Outdoor	Outdoors	Outings	Outside
Park	Patriotic	Perfect	Picnic	Picnic Basket
Picnic Blanket	Play	Playground	Pool	Poolside
Popsicle	Recreation	Red Hot	Refreshing	Relax
Relaxing	Rest	Ripe	Road Trip	Roasting

Rose	Sailing	Sandals	Sandcastle	Scorching
Sea	Searing Heat	Seashore	Season	Seasonal
Shade	Shaded	Swimsuit	Sunburn	Sun Burnt
Towel	Travel	Trip	Tropical	Visit

Describing Words for Autumn Season

Abundant	Acorn	Almond	Amber	Apple
Apple Cider	Apple Pie	Autumn	Autumnal	Autumnal Equinox
Back-To-School	Bale Of Hay	Bat	Blustery	Bountiful
Breezy	Bright	Brilliant	Brisk	Brown
Candy	Changing	Chestnut	Chestnuts	Chilly
Cider	Cobweb	Cold	Colder	Colored
Colorful	Colors	Columbus Day	Comfortable	Cool
Cooling	Corn	Corn Maze	Corn Stalk	Cornucopia
Costume	Country	Cozy	Crackling	Cranberry
Cranberries	Cranberry Sauce	Crisp	Crops	Crow
Crunchy	Deciduous	Earthy	Enchanting	Enjoyable
Fall	Fallen	Falling Leaves	Farmer	Feast
Festival	Fireside	Flannel	Fog	Foggy
Foliage	Football	Foraging	Fresh	Frost

Frosty	Fruit	Ghost	Gold	Golden
Gourd	Grain	Gray	Gusty	Halloween
Harvest	Harvested	Harvested	Harvest Moon	Hay
Hay Bale	Hayride	Hay Ride	Haystack	Hay Stack
Hibernating	Howling	Indian	Inspirational	Jack-O-Lantern
Leaf	Leaves	Leaf-Strewn	Magnificent	Maize
Maple	Mask	Mayflower	Migrate	Moonlit
Native American	November	Nuts	October	Orange
Overgrown	Pear	Pecan	Pecan Pie	Persimmon
Pilgrim	Pine Cone	Pumpkin	Pumpkin Bread	Pumpkin Pie
Quilt	Raincoat	Rainy	Rake	Raked
Reap	Red	Relaxing	Rice	Ripe
Roaring	Rust-Colored	Rustling	Scarecrow	Scarf
Scary	Season	Seasonal	Seeds	September
Sleet	Soggy	Spectacular	Spider	Spider's Web
Spooky	Squash	Squirrel	Stuffing	Sweater

Describing Words to Describe Family

WHAT'S YOUR PLAN ? A Pathway to Writing and Publishing Your Work

Absent-minded	Affectionate	Adventurous	Above-average	Unique
Balanced	Brave	Boisterous	Blunt	Beautiful
Bright	Cantankerous	Candid	Callous	Brilliant
Capable	Civil	Caustic	Careless	Careful
Clean	Cold	Coherent	Clumsy	Clever
Generous	Good	Glutinous	Gloomy	Gentle
Grave	Guarded	Grouchy	Groggy	Great
Cooperative	Crabby	Cowardly	Courageous	Cordial
Crafty	Mean	Mature	Crass	Cranky
Meddlesome	Hateful	Meticulous	Methodical	Mercurial
Hearty	Hypercritical	Hot-headed	Hesitant	Helpful
Hysterical	Musical	Motivated	Morose	Moronic
Superficial	Volcanic	Sweet	Suspicious	Surly
Stoic	Lame	Stupid	Strong	Striking
Lazy	Level-headed	Lethargic	Leery	Lean
Logical	Kind	Keen	Lovable	Long-winded
Irritating	Orderly	One-sided	Old-fashioned	Obnoxious
Ostentatious	Inspiring	Insensitive	Outspoken	Outgoing

Intelligent	Immature	Imaginative	Intolerant	Interesting
Impatient	Nervous	Negative	Nasty	Naive
Noisy	Quick	Querulous	Quarrelsome	Nosy
Quick-tempered	Talented	Tactless	Tactful	Quiet
Testy	Uncertain	Unbalanced	Unaffected	Ugly
Uncooperative	Unguarded	Unfriendly	Unemotional	Undependable
Unhelpful	Unpopular	Unpleasant	Unmotivated	Unimaginative
Unreliable	Wary	Warmhearted	Warm	Unsophisticated
Watchful	Well-intentioned	Well-developed	Well-behaved	Weak
Well-respected	Sensitive	Sensible	Selfish	Well-rounded
Sentimental	Shrewd	Short-tempered	Sharp	Serious
Shy	Spiteful	Spirited	Sour	Silly

Words to Describe a Best Friend

Affable	Available	Attentive	Amiable	Amicable
Awesome	Secluded	Outdoorsy	Quirky	Fantastic

Believable	Considerate	Cheerful	Caring	Brave
Bright	Sociable	Meticulous	Wide-eyed	Dense
Busy	Opportunistic	Exciting	Calm	Stereotypical
Centered	Golden	Compassionate	Understanding	Cuddly
Comforting	Diligent	Talkative	Vain	Unforgiving
Constant	Discerning	Generous	Sweet	Giving
Cordial	Forgiving	Faithful	Empathetic	Easygoing
Demanding	Energetic	Inquisitive	Sharp	Distant
Enthusiastic	Ambitious	Naïve	Warm	Calculating
Fun	Friendly	Reassuring	Dependable	Exciting
Gentle	Humorous	Heartfelt	Good-listener	Giving
Helpful	Articulate	Adventurous	Nice	Honest
Hungry	Forgetful	Worldly	Materialistic	Hard-working
Independent	Funny	Optimistic	Cool	Active
Lazy	Worrisome	Determined	Annoying	Witty
Loud	Fatherly	Motherly	Outspoken	Timid
Loving	Sensitive	Responsible	Reliable	Punctual

Outstanding	Exclusive	Merry-Weather	Off-Standish	Selfish
Righteous	Weird	Empathic	Supportive	Confident
Short	Conforming	Opinionated	Intelligent	Cute
Sincere	Trustworthy	Thoughtful	Sympathetic	Sociable
Strong	Creative	Kind	Assertive	Tolerant
Truthful	Cheerful	Tactful	Affectionate	Loyal
Truthful	Wonderful	Winning	Warm-hearted	Warm

Describing Words to Describe Nature

Void-Like	Enjoyable	Enchanting	Devoid	Colorful
Abloom	Anew	Alive	Airy	Active
Opulent	Blissful	Beautiful	Awakening	Paradisiac
Blooming	Bright	Breezy	Blossoming	Blue
Budding	Cheery	Cheerful	Changing	Buzzing
Chirping	Delightful	Crisp	Cloudless	Clean
Enjoyable	Flourishing	Floral	Fertile	Fair
Fragrant	Grassy	Gentle	Fresh	Free
Green	Healthy	Hatching	Happy	Growing

Heavenly	Joyful	Invigorating	Inspiring	Incredible
Light	Melting	Lush	Lovely	Lively
New	Peaceful	Pastel	Outdoor	Newborn
Picture-perfect	Pure	Pleasant	Pretty	Playing
Rainy	Renewing	Refreshing	Relaxing	Rejuvenating
Romping	Ethereal	Singing	Seasonal	Scampering
Beguiling	Special	Flawless	Soft	Breath-Taking
Ever-Changing	Sparkling	Sensuous	Awe-Inspiring	Unique
Spectacular	Sun-kissed	Sun-filled	Sprouting	Spring-inspired
Sunlit	Swimming	Sweet-smelling	Sweet	Sunny
Verdant	Teeming	Tender	Thriving	Unpredictable
Vernal	Young	Warming	Warm	Vibrant
Windy	Harsh	Vibrant	Woodland	Wondrous
Unforgiving	Spiritual	Inspirational	Earthy	Deciduous
Blazing	Wind-Swept	Bustling	Dreary	Desolate
Wooded	Picturesque	Crumbling	Towering	Derelict

Cobbled	Dense	Undulating	Massive	Expansive
Alluring	Dotted	Far-flung	Charming	Appealing
Mountainous	Breathtaking	Dusky	Ideal	Parched
Elegant	Fascinating	Exquisite	Barren	Sun-Drenched
Enticing	Quaint	Vivid	Arresting	Luscious

Describing Words to Describe "Life"

Radical	Terminal	Ultimate	Flawless	Twisted
Unappreciated	Beautiful	Subjective	Unfair	Taken-For-Granted
Progress	Relentless	Worthwhile	Painful	Ever-changing
Stable	Bewildering	Inspired	Unthinkable	Harsh
Confusing	Glorious	Overwhelming	Disappointing	Misleading
Superlative	Unbeatable	Untouchable	Unmatched	Grand
Outstanding	Delightful	Joyful	First-rate	First-class
Committed	Astonishing	Abundant	Unlimited	Impressive
Mind-	Extreme	Radiant	Awe-	Sensation

boggling			inspiring	al
Particular	Unrivaled	Unparalleled	Superb	Staggering
Supreme	Elated	Blissful	Indomitable	Invincible
Ecstatic	Horrible	Great	Fantastic	Jubilant
Magnificent	Fabulous	Stupendous	Stressful	Tiring
Incredible	Exceptional	Remarkable	Tremendous	Unbelievable
Phenomenal	Colossal	Awesome	Amazing	Extraordinary
Stunning	Abundant	Absolutely	Marvelous	Prodigious
Accept	Action-Packed	Achievement	Accomplishment	Acclaimed
Active	Astounding	Adventure	Acumen	Activist
Astute	Bountiful	Beautiful	Basic	Authentic
Brave	Charming	Charitable	Bubbly	Brilliant
Cherished	Complete	Companionship	Commend	Classy
Comradeship	Content	Constant	Connected	Confident
Copious	Creative	Courageous	Coupled	Core
Cultivate	Delightful	Dazzling	Cute	Curious
Discovery	Encompas	Elegance	Electrifying	Distinguis

	sing			hed
Established	Legendary	Ideal	Genuine	Full
Metamorphosis	Rich	Rewarding	Purposeful	Positive
Spirited	Unwavering	Unusual	Spontaneous	Splendid
Voyage	Wondrous	Wholesome	Whole	Wealthy
Young	Dull	Zesty	Zingy	Zestful

Describing Words to Describe "Style"

Bold	Vivid	Distinctive	Crazy	Hot
Sophisticated	Amazing	Creative	Innovative	Dynamic
Sweet	Trend	Beauty	Free	Ambitious
Standout	Simple	Chic	Creative	Colorful
Cute	Crisp	Conversational	Circuitous	Ever-changing
Clean	Economical	Discursive	Diffuse	Declamatory
Elliptical	Epigrammatic	Emphatic	Expressing	Eloquent
Epistolary	Formal	Fluent	Flowery	Euphemistic
Gossipy	Inarticulate	Ruddy	Idiomatic	Grandiloqu

WHAT'S YOUR PLAN? A Pathway to Writing and Publishing Your Work

Incoherent	Learned	Journalistic	Informal	Unable ent
Learned	Ornate	Lyrical	Orotund	Lyric
Parenthetical	Poetic	Pithy	Picturesque	Pejorative
Polemical	Punchy	Prolix	Portentous	Ponderous
Rambling	Shakespearean	Sesquipedalian	Rhetorical	Readable
Slangy	Unprintable	Turgid	Succinct	Stylistic
Literary	Worded	Well-turned	Verbose	Vague
Wordy	Cheap	Timid	Loud	Outspoken
Flamboyant	Frugal	Grating	Clingy	Annoying
Approach	Design	Description	Characteristic	Behavior
Form	Method	Kind	Habit	Genre
Mode	Tone	Technique	Spirit	Pattern
Trend	Custom	Bearing	Appearance	Variety
Flashy	Unwavering	Peculiarity	Idiosyncrasy	Groovy
Blissful	Eager	Romantic	Shameless	Astonishing
Strong	Stunning	Scary	Giddy	Rich
Daunting	Surprising	Challenging	Sensual	Illogical

Fresh	Communication	Respect	Loving	Bold
Loyalty	Capable	Charismatic	Cute	Captivating
Smart	Snug	Sensitive	Sophisticated	Spellbinding
Satisfying	Sexy	Smoldering	Superb	Steadfast

Describing Words to Describe a Hero

Courageous	Responsible	Dedicated	Compassionate	Selfless
Valorous	Charismatic	Disciplined	Intelligent	Trustworthy
Loyal	Ingenious	Determined	Caring	Kind
Faithful	Relentless	Noble	Inspiring	Generous
Fearless	Moral	Strong	Valiant	Self-sacrificing
Wise	Bold	Humble	Clever	Daring
Virtuous	Benevolent	Altruistic	Sincere	Honorable
Bighearted	Gracious	Free	Considerate	Chivalrous
Greathearted	Princely	Magnanimous	Lofty	Liberal

ted		us		
Unselfish	Courageous	Aweless	Audacious	Assuming
Witty	Dauntless	Enterprising	Gallant	Intrepid
Resolute	Defiant	Dashing	Daring	Confident
Doughty	Forward	Foolhardy	Firm	Fearless
Game	Imprudent	Hardy	Gutsy	Gritty
Indomitable	Plucky	Nervy	Militant	Lionhearted
Reckless	Stouthearted	Stout	Stalwart	Spirited
Unabashed	Undismayed	Undaunted	Unflinching	Unafraid
Unfearful	Spunky	Cheeky	Venturesome	Cocky
Inspiring	Commanding	Knowledgeable	Dominating	Role-Models
Dignified	Excellent	Exalted	Eminent	Distinguished
Leader	Talented	Renowned	Prominent	Idealist
Hidden	Proud	Tough	Herculean	Stately
Storied	Prodigious	Imposing	Extraordinary	Celebrated
Adventurous	Admirable	Protectors	Persevering	Tenacious
Outstandi	Strong-	Powerful	Unshakeabl	Brassy

ng	Willed		e
Worthy	Witty		

Describing Words That Describe "Pain"

Achy	Chapped	Bad		Agony	Agonizing
Chapped	Excruciating	Dull		Crippling	Chronic
Gnawing	Continuously	Gripping		Heavy	Inflamed
Irritated	Severe	Raw		Raging	Itchy
Sore	Uncomfortable	Stabbing		Sudden	Stiff
Stinging	Torturous	Tight		Thumping	Tender
Physical	Unendurable	Holding		Vice-like	Unpleasant
Squeezing	Excruciatingly	Agonizingly	Painful		Violent
Tingling	Numbing	Sharp		Shooting	Throbbing
Piercing	Pounding	Intermittent		Crawling	Crushing
Tearing	Sensenational	Discomfort		Fever	Illness

Describing Words to Describe a "Man"

Accomplished	Accountable	Active	Admirable	Adventurous
Affectionate	Aggressive	Agreeable	Ambitious	Analytical
Appreciated	Appreciative	Articulate	Artistic	Assertive
Athletic	Brave	Authoritative	Attractive	Attentive
Brawny	Calculating	Busy	Brilliant	Bright
Charismatic	Classy	Chivalrous	Chiseled	Charming
Clever	Commanding	Committed	Compassionate	Competitive
Complex	Confident	Conservative	Courageous	Daring
Dashing	Demanding	Determined	Devilish	Devoted
Devout	Dignified	Disciplined	Distinguished	Dominant
Driven	Dynamic	Easy-going	Educated	Effective
Entertaining	Fit	Fearless	Fatherly	Enthusiastic
Focused	Friendly	Funny	Handsome	Hardworking
Healthy	Hilarious	High-	Heroic	Helpful

		energy		
Honest	Hot	Humble	Inspiring	Intellectual
Intelligent	Intuitive	Kind	Kind-hearted	Kingly
Logical	Lovable	Loving	Loyal	Magnetic
Mature	Mechanical	Observant	Offbeat	Outgoing
Passionate	Paternal	Playful	Poetic	Poised
Polished	Positive	Powerful	Practical	Principled
Professional	Quirky	Quiet	Quick-witted	Punctual
Radical	Rebellious	Refined	Resourceful	Respectable
Romantic	Rough	Rugged	Sacrificing	Scholarly
Scrappy	Sculpted	Secure	Seductive	Sensitive
Serious	Sexual	Sexy	Sharp	Shrewd
Shy	Single-minded	Smart	Social	Sophisticated
Spontaneous	Stocky	Stern	Statuesque	Stable
Strapping	Talented	Tactful	Successful	Suave
Thick-skinned	Thorough	Thoughtful	Unique	Upbeat
Valiant	Visionary	Warm	Wealthy	Youthful

Describing Words to Describe "Food"

Peppery	Bubbly	Browned	Seasoned	Skunky
Burning	Canned	Candied	Buttery	Bursting
Caramelized	Charred	Charioteer	Chalky	Caustic
Cheesy	Chewy	Chili	Chilled	Chipotle
Chocolaty	Classical	Clarified	Chowder	Chopped
Condensed	Creamery	Creamed	Course	Condiment
Creamy	Creole	Crispy	Crumbly	Crunchy
Crusty	Curdled	Curd	Cuisine	Crystalized
Cured	Deglazed	Decadent	Dash	Curried
Dehydrated	Deveined	Delightful	Delicious	Delectable
Deviled	Disagreeable	Dipping	Diluted	Dietary
Disgusting	Dredged	Divine	Distinctive	Distasteful
Drenched	Dry-Roasted	Drizzled	Dry	Dripping
Dull	Dusted	Earthy	Succulent	Edible
Enjoyable	Enticing	Entrée	Escalloped	Evaporated
Exquisite	Fermented	Fine	Fibrous	Filling
Fiery	Fishy	Fizzy	Flakey	Flavorless
Flavorsome	Florentine	Floury	Fluffy	Folded
Foul	Bland	Fragrant	Feathery	Fresh
Freeze-dried	Fricasseed	Fried	Frosty	Frozen
Fruity	Full-bodied	Full-flavored	Gamy	Garlicky

Gingery	Glazed	Good	Gooey	Grainy
Granulated	Grated	Gratifying	Greasy	Griddled
Grilled	Gritty	Gross	Hard-boiled	Heady
Heat	Heavy	Healthy	Heavenly	Hearty
Hint	Homogenized	Honeyed	Hot	Boring
Icy	Infused	Intense	Inviting	Juicy
Julienne	Kosher	Laced	Laden	Layered
Lemony	Light	Limp	Lip-smacking	Liquid
Low-Fat	Blanched	Steamed	Lumpy	Acidic

ABOUT THE AUTHOR

Alberta Lampkins is the Publisher of A.L. Savvy Publications, an independent publishing company established in 2014. She is the Author of the book, *Teach Me How To Fly* and Project coordinator and contributing author of the book, *Messages to Our Children.* She is an avid reader and the President of the, Dazzling Divas Literary Club.

Alberta holds a B.A. and a M.A. Degree in Sociology from Fayetteville State University. She is the mother of two adult children, Alexis and Ahmad and the proud grandmother of Elijah. She is a native of Buffalo, New York, but currently resides in New Jersey with her husband CSM Albert Lampkins.

Notes

ALBERTA LAMPKINS

WHAT'S YOUR PLAN ? A Pathway to Writing and Publishing Your Work

WHAT'S YOUR PLAN ? A Pathway to Writing and Publishing Your Work

www.ingramcontent.com/pod-product-compliance
Lightning Source LLC
Chambersburg PA
CBHW070528010526
44110CB00049B/1435